VOLUNTEERS
CRIMINAL JUSTICE
SYSTEM

VOLUNTEERS IN THE CRIMINAL JUSTICE SYSTEM

A comparative study of probation, police and victim support

M. L. GILL and R. I. MAWBY

OPEN UNIVERSITY PRESS
Milton Keynes • Philadelphia

Open University Press
Celtic Court
22 Ballmoor
Buckingham
MK18 1XW

and
1900 Frost Road, Suite 101
Bristol, PA 19007, USA

First Published 1990

British Library Cataloguing in Publication Data

Gill, M. L. (Martin L.)
    Volunteers in the criminal justice system: a comparative
study of probation, police, and victim support.
    1. Great Britain. Voluntary welfare work
    I. Title   II. Mawby, R. I. (Rob I)
    361.7′0941

    ISBN 0 335 15880 3
          0 335 15879 X (pbk)

Library of Congress Cataloging-in-Publication Data

Gill, M. L.
    Volunteers in the criminal justice system: a comparative study of
    probation, police and victim support / M. L. Gill and R. I. Mawby.
        p.   cm.
    Includes bibliographical references.
    ISBN 0–335–15880–3. – ISBN 0–335–15879–X (pbk.)
    1. Volunteer workers in criminal justice administration – Great
    Britain. I. Mawby, R. I.   II. Title.
    HV9960.G7G55   1990
    364.6 – dc20   89–22986 CIP

Typeset by Scarborough Typesetting Services
Printed in Great Britain by Biddles Ltd
Guildford and Kings Lynn

CONTENTS

LIST OF TABLES

LIST OF FIGURES

PREFACE

There are many people who deserve a sign of gratitude for their co-operation in this study, most of whom by necessity must remain nameless. In particular we mean here the numerous volunteers, professionals and other workers who answered our questions enthusiastically, not least because they frequently indicated that it has been a largely unexamined and neglected field of inquiry. We thank them for helping us to move towards rectifying this deficiency.

More generally, thanks are due to the Devon and Cornwall Probation Services; the Devon and Cornwall Police and victim support schemes in the two counties. Our liaisons here were respectively Gordon Read, Tony North, Roy Acton and Pauline Letteridge, and all that follows is indicative of the truly efficient and effective role they played, not only as liaisons but as advisers too.

To the typists involved in aiding with the various drafts we offer both apologies and thanks at the same time: apologies for the (lack of) quality of handwriting (especially of one of us) and thanks for carrying on the good work regardless. We are also grateful to our academic colleagues for their varying contributions.

Finally: this is the second time we have collaborated on a book, and we can confirm that it does not get any easier. Altering each other's drafts, discussing and even arguing over theoretical and practical points are probably a prerequisite for progress, although it does not always seem so at the time. Nevertheless, as we part as friends and prepare for another venture, we are mindful of the fact that until we are advised of an alternative the best way to proceed is to contend every last damn word.

Martin Gill
Rob Mawby

1 | COMMUNITY INVOLVEMENT IN THE CRIMINAL JUSTICE SYSTEM

INTRODUCTION

Discussions of the role of the public, or the community, in the criminal justice system raise mixed emotions. We may feel that a system of justice, subject to the rule of law, should be controlled by professionals who are accountable for their decisions, but we also perhaps wonder if a system which excludes the public from involvement is ineffective and open to abuse. We acknowledge that community participation was greater in pre-industrial societies, but we recognize the importance of maintaining some level of community involvement.

The role of the public, and the community, in the criminal justice system has received surprisingly little systematic evaluation. Yet the public do participate in a variety of ways. A review of statistics on the criminal justice system gives some indication of levels of public involvement. Although in a minority, volunteers operate alongside the police and the probation service, including work in prisons. Moreover, the criminal courts provide employment for less than a thousand judges, recorders, registrars and paid or stipendiary magistrates whose numbers are dwarfed by the 21,000 or so volunteer magistrates who give their time to preside over the magistrates courts (Central Statistical Office 1988). And, of course, the work of such courts would be considerably less should the public, as victims or witnesses, choose not to involve the police by reporting crime or by supplying evidence to support the prosecution.

Where magistrates are not involved in decision making, in the Crown Courts, citizen participation is introduced through the jury system where public involvement is *required*. Although a smaller *proportion* of cases are tried before a jury than in the past, the increased volume of criminal-court work means that more cases are heard by a jury than before (Simon 1980), and despite current criticisms of jury composition and alleged irrational decision making (Ingman

1987), the principle of public participation through the jury system, a principle which can be traced back to at least the twelfth century, remains sacrosanct. For example:

> Let it not be supposed that this court is in any way opposed to trial by jury. It has been the bulwark of our liberties too long for any of us to seek to alter it.
> (Lord Denning, quoted in R. H. Jackson 1979: 483)

> Trial by jury is more than an instrument of justice and more than one wheel of the constitution; it is the lamp that shows that freedom lives.
> (Devlin 1956: 164)

Of course, jury service, unlike most other public involvement, is not voluntary. There are numerous other differences between different types of public participation. One distinction, made by Wolfenden (1978), is between informal involvement and voluntary work as part of some organized group. Another is in terms of the *extent* of participation. Citizen involvement for a few minutes in deciding to report a crime; participation on a panel of jurists for perhaps one week; these are examples of minimal involvement. At the other extreme, neighbourhood-watch co-ordinators, probation volunteers, magistrates or victim-support volunteers, may devote hours of every week as unpaid participants in the criminal justice system. Why do they give so much of their time? How useful and distinctive is their contribution? The remainder of this book is an attempt at spelling out levels of community involvement and its outcome. In attempting such a broad task we have focused in detail on three groups of volunteers, those working with the probation service, the police (as special constables) and victim-support schemes, and these form the main parts of our studies reported in Chapters 3–7.

Before we concentrate on these three groups, however, it is instructive to look at community involvement in a wider context, and this we have attempted to do in the remainder of this chapter and Chapter 2. Thus we begin, at the beginning, with a brief historical review of community involvement in law and order, and a summary of more recent developments in the post-war period. We then introduce an international dimension by citing research on community participation in the criminal justice systems of other countries. Then in the final section to this chapter we consider the current appeal of community involvement.

Chapter 2 approaches the topic from a slightly different direction. First, we draw a distinction between community involvement in an informal sense and voluntary work as a more formalized and organized basis for participation. We then focus on voluntarism, by synthesizing material on the criminal justice system with lessons from the wider voluntary welfare sector. Thus we consider different types of voluntary organization and volunteers and introduce a number of claims made either on behalf of or in criticism of the voluntary sector. These discussions are then used as the platform for our own research in subsequent chapters. Before that, however, we shall consider volunteering in the broader sense of community involvement, starting with the situation in Britain some one thousand years ago.

A BRIEF HISTORY OF COMMUNITY INVOLVEMENT

Police historians such as Critchley (1978) have singled out Anglo-Saxon England as epitomizing a criminal justice system based on local groups' responsibilities. Groups of ten families were bound together to form a *tything*, which was the basic unit for administrative responsibilities such as tax collection and law enforcement. The *tything* had corporate responsibility for the actions of its members and, should anyone commit a crime, the others were legally obliged to produce him for trial. The elected leader of the *tything* was responsible to a *hundredman* who himself reported to the *shire reeve* or sheriff, who could, in an emergency, call on the ancient system of 'hue and cry' and call a *posse*. For the most part, however, crimes were handled by the *shire reeve* on a local level, with the offender paying compensation (*wer* or *bot*) to the victim and a fine (*wite*) to the lord (Fry 1951: 28–30).

Although this system was located within the local community, it was, as Brogden *et al.* (1988) observe, scarcely *controlled* by the citizens themselves; it was imposed on behalf of the local lord, to ensure that his land was maintained in a profitable and orderly fashion. However, the Norman invasion signalled a shift towards more central control. The system, renamed *frankpledge*, required the sheriffs, as royal office holders, to conduct courts on a twice-yearly basis, at which the *tything* relationships were reconfirmed and small group issues could be assessed at this higher level. Following the Assize of Clarendon in 1166, *tythingmen* were required to recount at these regular courts any rumours or suspicions to a twelve-man jury, which then referred any serious issues to the sheriff. However, as Stead (1985) rightly observes, although the system hinged around the sheriffs, as royal officials, at local level it depended on ordinary citizens, a departure from the Roman model of paid officials.

Three levels of local involvement were central to the system which emerged between the twelfth and fourteenth centuries – the jury, the constables and the justices. The former was originally a group of peers who provided local information on those involved in disputes. By the mid-fourteenth century, however, juries were responsible for verdicts and the principle of a unanimous verdict had been established (Smith and Bailey 1984: 607).

Constables were appointed annually, along with mayors and bailiffs, as unpaid local community leaders. The Statute of Winchester (1285) confirmed their responsibilities and those of other citizens and created for the towns a back-up system of night-time watchmen, in which all adult males were required to participate (Critchley 1978).

Justices, created through the Justices of the Peace Act (1361), provided an essential centralizing component to supplement the local arrangements of the Statute of Winchester. At county level, responsibility for upholding the king's peace was placed in the hands of 'one Lord, and with him three or four of the most worthy in the county'. These justices, clearly socially superior to the constables, thus become responsible for law within the county and administered it at parish level through the local, annually appointed constables (Critchley 1978; Milton 1967; Smith and Bailey 1984).

With minor modifications, this system operated until well into the eighteenth century. Its demise is the matter of some controversy (Brogden *et al.* 1988). However it appears that the social and economic conditions (including widening class divisions) of industrializing and more urban-based society made it less viable and made voluntary offices less desirable. For example, those who could afford to avoided their term of duty as constable or watchman by paying a substitute. Defoe, perhaps the most commonly cited example, paid £10 in 1721 to be excused his duties in Stoke Newington. Equally, it became increasingly difficult in some areas to find competent and (politically) reliable members of the local gentry who could take on the responsibility as magistrates (Smith and Bailey 1984). By the time of the Chartist disturbances of the 1830s for example, it was precisely those areas where social order was most threatened where upper- or middle-class support in law-enforcement duties was least evident (Mather 1959).

What emerged by the early nineteenth century can thus best be described as a mixed economy of criminal justice with considerable local variation and little in the way of central control. In many areas community-based systems still prevailed, supported perhaps by more formal voluntary organizations such as local law-and-order pressure groups like the Associations for the Prosecution of Felons (Shubert 1981) or the yeomanry, a middle-class volunteer militia occasionally used in times of disorder (Mather 1959). However, to a large extent 'obligation' was replaced by the profit motive. Thus some were attracted to law enforcement by the financial reward to be gained, by charging public or prisoners for services within or above the course of duty, pocketing fines, or acting as bounty hunters and living from the proceeds of the various rewards for the arrest of offenders or return of stolen property (Ericson *et al.* 1987; Radzinowicz 1956a; Spitzer and Scull 1977). Others were formally employed to carry out law-enforcement duties, by private citizens (or groups of local residents), private companies, or the government. Nineteenth-century reform of the criminal justice system, notably central- or local-government control of the police, prisons and courts (Critchley 1978; Hart 1955, 1956; Radzinowicz 1956a, 1956b; P. T. Smith 1985; Steedman 1984; Thomas 1972), thus brought statutory control to a patchwork of services, among which local community control had lost much of its earlier significance.

The last vestiges of community involvement in criminal justice were, arguably, to be found in the magistracy and the jury. Yet each, significantly, was a middle- or upper-class preserve. Magistrates had, of course, always been high-status, politically reliable 'representatives' (at least in name) of the community. This was legally confirmed through property qualification, raised to £100 in 1732 and not abolished until 1906 (R. H. Jackson 1979: 288). Similarly juries became distanced from their communities. By the eighteenth century, for example, it was established that a juror would be excluded from any case of which he had personal knowledge, and only a property-owning minority were eligible for jury service (R. H. Jackson 1979; Smith and Bailey 1984). Indeed, writing in the early nineteenth century, de Tocqueville described the institution of the English jury as aristocratic rather than democratic (Simon 1980: 6). Moreover, what voluntary organizations emerged at the time, such as the various Associations for the Prosecution of Felons (Mather 1959; Shubert 1981) and the John Howard Society (Ryan 1978) were essentially middle class.

Overall however, with perhaps the notable exception of voluntary movements directed at saving the destitute or delinquent young (Pinchbeck and Hewitt 1973) and probation (see page 30) it seems that in Britain the voluntary sector played a less significant role than the private one in the transition from a community-based to a statutory criminal justice system. Unlike the welfare system, the voluntary sector was more involved in pressure-group activities than in service deliveries.

THE REBIRTH OF THE VOLUNTARY SECTOR

In contrast to the criminal justice system, the development of the welfare state in Britain was preceded by a complex and widespread network of voluntary services in the nineteenth century. As the importance of welfare based in the local community – and orchestrated by church and gentry – declined, so early state initiatives were overshadowed by the voluntary sector as the middle classes of Victorian England buried their guilt in good works and headed off potential revolution by smoothing the jagged edges of capitalism's flotsam. Many early attempts at social reform focused on children, most readily recognized as deserving cases, and were reflected in organizations such as the YMCA, Barnardo's, and the Waifs and Strays Society, and legislation restricting child exploitation (Hobhouse 1939; Pinchbeck and Hewitt 1973; Simeral 1916; Walvin 1982). However, as the role of the state in the provision of welfare services became more pronounced in the early twentieth century and again in the 1940s, the role of the voluntary sector subsided, to the point where some questioned whether it would survive (Brasnett 1969). Indeed, the two major post-war reports on volunteers (Aves 1969) and voluntary organizations (Wolfenden 1978) took place in an environment of pessimism and contraction, reflected in the reports' need to justify a distinctive place for the voluntary sector.

Within the criminal justice system, the voluntary sector had never had such a broad base. True, many of the early initiatives to 'save' children became formalized as charities, and the probation service developed from the earlier voluntary work of the London Court Missionaries. However, as we shall show later, use of volunteers by both probation and police was rarely systematic or well planned. Perhaps the most significant voluntary agency operating within the criminal justice system was the National Association of Discharged Prisoners' Aid Societies (NADPAS). Until incorporated into the probation service in the mid-1960s, NADPAS co-ordinated the work of local voluntary organizations with regard to prison welfare and after-care services. This apart, the most significant intrusion of the public into the system was within the courts, with lay magistrates predominating in the lower courts, and – in a rather different sense but reflecting the public voice – the jury held sacred in the higher courts.

Lay magistrates are in fact appointed by the Lord Chancellor in consultation with local advisory committees and thus constitute a chosen few among many potential volunteers. Their membership is no longer restricted by a property qualification, but studies have demonstrated their social distance from the public they allegedly represent. A Royal Commission in 1948 showed magistrates to be dominated by professional and managerial classes (Smith and Bailey 1984: 136–7), Hood's (1972) research some twenty years later revealed little change, and Baldwin (1976) subsequently noted that a shift towards more lower middle- and working-class male magistrates was more than counteracted by an increase in female members of the bench who were even more disproportionately from the higher social classes. The same studies have found magistrates to be relatively old and predominantly male. Although recent policies have aimed at increasing the proportions of younger, female and working-class representatives, as well as minority groups, it is evident that the overall composition remains essentially unchanged. The same appears true in Scotland, where a slightly different system operates (Bankowski et al. 1987).

This is less true of jury composition. Until 1972 the jury list was based on a property rateable-value criterion, resulting in the typical jury being 'predominantly male, middle-age, middle-minded and middle-class' (Devlin 1956: 20). As R. H. Jackson (1979: 487) recalls:

A few years before the war I took as a sample a ward in Cambridge that consisted partly of working-class houses, old and new, and partly of middle-class houses. There were just under 5,000 parliamentary electors, and the list showed 187 jurors, which works out roughly at one juror to every 26 electors. It was only by some stretch of the imagination that a working-class prisoner could be said to be tried by 'twelve representatives of his countrymen'.

In response to growing criticisms, the electoral register was adopted as the basis for qualification in 1972. As a result, juries have tended to be younger and less middle class, although women and racial minorities still appear under-represented (Baldwin and McConville 1979). Indeed, it may be the increased representativeness of the jury which has led to many recent criticisms of it! (See Findlay and Duff 1988; Ingman 1987; Smith and Bailey 1984.)

In fact, the jury system symbolizes for many the importance of retaining a role for the public in the criminal justice system. But what of other forms of longer-term public commitment?

Perhaps the most significant development in the 1960s was the creation of the National Association for the Care and Resettlement of Offenders (NACRO) in 1966 (following the demise of NADPAS), combining at least two roles as a service provider and pressure group and reflecting similar movements elsewhere in the voluntary sector towards national 'umbrella' co-ordinating bodies. In welfare terms, though, the 1970s were a major period for growth, both of older, traditional-type voluntary agencies and new forms focusing more on self-help, pressure-group activities, community involvement, and consumer rights (Hatch 1980). Within the criminal justice system, these were reflected in the birth of Radical Alternatives to Prison (RAP) (Ryan 1978) and the prisoners' rights organization, PROP. Similarly, as we have detailed elsewhere (Mawby and Gill 1987: 75–86), this was also the period during which refuges for battered women were opened, first in Chiswick and subsequently under the umbrella of the Federation of Women's Aid Groups, and rape crisis centres were also started up, partly influenced by initiatives in North America. Also in the mid-1970s victim support was created with the opening of the Bristol Victims Support Scheme in 1974–5 (Mawby and Gill 1987: 87–90).

These expansions have, however, been given increased impetus by government initiatives of the 1980s. Rather than voluntary services being seen as redundant in an age of increased statutory involvement, current government enthusiasm for a minimum state has led to a resurgence of interest in the voluntary sector and other alternatives. Before describing the main thrusts behind such initiatives, however, it is useful to draw in some international comparisons in order to illustrate the alternative roles which the community might play in the criminal justice system of a complex industrial society.

COMMUNITY INVOLVEMENT ABROAD

It is tempting to accept the generalized assumption that as societies become more complex and incorporate a refined division of labour, so their legal systems will become more specialist and professional, and the role of the community will shrink. There is certainly evidence of this from analysis of a range of non-industrial societies (Schwartz and Miller 1964). Bayley (1985) associates industrialization with the emergence of centralized, professional, specialist law enforcement, and a medley of authors have commented on the resultant, near universal banishment of the victim from direct involvement in court decision making (Gittler 1984; Harding 1982; MacDonald 1976; Schafer 1960).

Yet within this broad pattern there are noticeable differences of emphasis. For example, countries more heavily influenced by Roman law and government tended to incorporate centralized specialists at an earlier stage (Bayley 1985); the centrally controlled French system is a good example, with the development of a specialist co-ordinated system of law enforcement in the period of Louis XIV in the mid-seventeenth century (Emsley 1983). On the other hand, British colonial influence, especially involving the subordination of native populations, led to more centralized systems based on the Irish model rather than that of mainland Britain (Brogden 1987), in some cases accelerating the demise of earlier communal systems (Griffiths 1971).

The North American system of criminal justice is interesting in a number of respects, incorporating as it did many of the features of the English system of the eighteenth century. The jury system, for example, was transposed (with some apparent flexibility over the optimum number of jurors) and, despite claims that it was more democratic than its English forebear, similarly excluded non-property owners, females and racial minorities. It did, however, serve a popular function in allowing the laws of England to be re-interpreted to serve the interests of a society moving towards independence (Hyman and Tarrant 1975; Simon 1980). It is also sometimes asserted that the American public prosecutor emerged as a professional heir to the English justices (Gittler 1984: 127). In general terms though, the American system of justice which developed reflected other public services within a federation of states (Heidenheimer et al. 1983), resisted centralization, and indeed at local level incorporated more community ties than was the case in England (Miller 1977), as it moved from an 'antiquated watch-and-ward system (daytime constables and nightime watchmen)' (Brown 1969a: 60) to a modern urban policing system. Moreover, public attempts to retain control over law and order were directly expressed in a series of vigilante campaigns which drew strength from either the lack of an effective system of justice or citizen rejection of the system currently operating (Brown 1969a, 1969b; Frantz 1969).

But what of countries other than those from the Western capitalist bloc? Japan is an interesting example of alternative developments within capitalism. On the one hand it features a bureaucratic, central state, which is partly a reflection of Confucianism (Fulcher 1988), partly, in the context of policing, attributable to the French and German traditions influential in its formative years (Ames 1981; McKensie 1984). On the other hand, central administration traditionally permeates local neighbourhoods through a series of complex networks, and community involvement in crime control and dispute resolution (as well as street cleaning), within very small urban neighbourhoods, is more complex and more involved than in other capitalist societies (Alderson 1981a; Ames 1979, 1981; Bayley 1976; Clifford 1976).

Socialist societies display equal variance. There is a marked distinction between those which have adopted the Eastern European model of centralized, bureaucratic government and those which have prioritized grassroots involvement, a distinction evident across a broad range of public and social policy areas (Deacon 1983; White and Nelson 1986). Countries such as the USSR have allowed some devolution of power to the local level – factory or neighbourhood – in some respects, but in the context of criminal justice this has tended to involve rather peripheral areas of deviance (Armstrong 1967; Karpets 1977; O'Connor

1964). In contrast, alternative forms are evident in countries such as Cuba and China (particularly under Mao). In Cuba, for example, during the 1960s, the formal court structure was to a large extent replaced by popular tribunals, or people's courts, often held in the open, at which local representatives presided over a motley of work and neighbourhood participants who 'spontaneously' provided details of the case under consideration (Berman 1969; Salas 1979, 1985). Equally, at grass-roots level, during the 1960s a majority of the population aged over 14 were involved in community groups instigated by Castro, such as the Committees for the Defence of the Revolution, which were involved in organizing censuses, patrol and guard duty and in co-ordinating information for pre-sentence or bail investigations (Binns and Gonzalez 1980; Salas 1979). In China similarly, Mao's concern to avoid centralized bureaucratic control led to the encouragement of community-based mediation structures (Cohen 1971; Lubman 1967, 1969) and the involvement of the community in policing through residents' groups and Security Defence Small Groups (Alderson 1981a; Cohen 1968; Vogel 1971).

While in general terms, then, community involvement in criminal justice is less pronounced in more industrialized societies, socialist or capitalist, there are considerable variations. Japan is a good illustration of a developed capitalist society where community involvement is extensive, and Cuba provides an example of community involvement encouraged (or imposed) by a revolutionary regime where there was no prior tradition of such involvement. Moreover, these very different examples suggest that the perceived advantages of community involvement may be many and varied. With this in mind, we can return to a consideration of recent initiatives in Britain.

PUBLIC PARTICIPATION: CURRENT ISSUES

In the following chapter we shall discuss some of the main benefits and problems with the voluntary sector. Here, by way of introduction, we wish to identify some current issues surrounding the more general theme of community involvement. Where there is overlap, we have chosen to leave the discussion until later.

Critiques of an over-reliance on professionals and advocacy of community involvement, while closely identified with the present government in Britain, are clearly not monopolized by the right. The self-help movement which heralded the rejuvenation of voluntarism in the 1970s, illustrated on an international stage by the writings of Ivan Illich, is one example of its wider appeal (Illich 1973; Illich et al. 1977) as was the strategy adopted by the Labour-controlled GLC in London (Sheard 1986). Similarly, in a comparison of welfare systems under socialism, Deacon (1983) argues for greater levels of public participation and the breaking down of professional barriers.

Perhaps not surprisingly then, current thinking on the role of the public in the criminal justice system is diverse. Nevertheless, we can identify a number of strands, although these are not mutually exclusive. The first of these is the philosophy of minimal government. This has been dominant in Britain following the election of Margaret Thatcher in 1979 and is echoed in North America (Ericson *et al.* 1987). Behind curtailed commitment to state provision rests expectations that a stronger mixed economy of welfare – that is the family, community, voluntary and private sector – will plug the gaps. In an address to the National Conference of the Women's Royal Voluntary Service in 1981, the Prime Minister presented her own blueprint for the ideal statutory–voluntary partnership:

> I am very encouraged by the way in which local authorities' directors of social services, the social work profession and the specialist press are increasingly determined to shift the emphasis of voluntary provision so that it becomes an enabling service, a statutory provision enabling the volunteers to do their job more effectively.
>
> (Thatcher 1981)

This view to some extent paralleled that of the Barclay (1982) Committee in its identification of the future structure of social services departments. However, despite an acceptance by the Home Office (1984) that probation could also prioritize community involvement, it appeared that government initiatives might largely pass by the criminal justice system. True, encouragement has been given to the development of private-sector prisons, advocated in a report by the Centre for Policy Studies (Pirie and Young 1987: 26), and by the Parliamentary Expenditure Committee (House of Commons 1987). Similarly there are those who advocate privatization of some police functions (Hoare 1988).

A key issue behind policies of a restricted role for the state is the financial benefits in alternative provisions. There are several strands which are of importance here, and these will be discussed more fully later in the context of the voluntary sector. It should, however, be noted that the time taken by professionals to 'organize' the community to become involved may eat away at advantages in terms of cost (Haxby 1978). Similarly on the level of the organization, the belief that voluntary services are cheaper than statutory services is tainted by two considerations: that costs are cheaper because wages are lower, and that the voluntary sector evidences increasing reliance on the state for finance (Brenton 1985).

Nevertheless, the appeal to the community attracts far more support than it would as a merely cynical means of cutting the costs of state involvement. Another argument is that community involvement is essentially preferable to state dependency. This statement is explicit in the work of Illich, the Barclay Report, and the Home Office policy statement on probation, but perhaps finds most expression in the reaction in United States to the Kitty Genovese homicide (Rosenthal 1964). Kitty Genovese was the victim of a brutal, noisy, and somewhat prolonged murder near her apartment. What promoted the case to front-page news, however, was the subsequent discovery that no less than 38 individuals heard the victim call out for help, but no one responded, even by calling the police, until it was too late. When interviewed later, most excused themselves on the grounds that they felt that it was the job of the police to deal with crime; in other words, crime prevention was for the paid experts, not a community responsibility.

The case provoked a number of research studies, many by psychologists, attempting to explain bystander inaction (Latane and Darley 1970: for a review see Mawby 1985). Common to these and to wider public reaction was the view that the community does indeed have a part to play, and a society in which help is seen as someone else's responsibility is undesirable. Threads of such a view are, equally, to be found in works advocating neighbourhood watch and victim support (NAVSS 1982: 22).

Similar arguments in favour of community involvement within the court setting have been made by Pitts (1988). The author suggests that juvenile courts should be replaced by lay tribunals through a 'civilization' process and observes:

> An appearance at a community court, facing neighbours and being asked to justify one's actions to them may well be more effective than punishment. Such a process also gives community representation a chance to confront those who have offended them and express a justifiable anger which probably has more meaning than the incomprehensible rituals of the formal court appearance.
>
> (Pitts 1988: 164)

Along similar lines, alternatives to state provision are seen as essential ingredients of democracy allowing all to participate in society (Beveridge and Wells 1949; Hatch 1980). It is at the same time a means by which citizens' rights are protected from powerful occupational or professional élites. The limited extent to which agencies such as the police are accountable to the public they allegedly serve was thus used by Lord Scarman (1981) to advocate wider community involvement, a case argued by a variety of academics (see for example Kinsey et al. 1986; Morgan 1987), as well as some practitioners (Alderson 1981b). In policing terms it is illustrated in the emergence, with government encouragement, of community consultative groups (Fyfe 1987) and lay visitors (Walklate 1987), but it is also reflected in earlier concerns over the continuance of the jury system, the operation of parole (Stern 1987) and social control in prison (Maguire and Vagg 1984). Of course, as we shall note in more detail later, this raises the question of the social characteristics of those members of the public who are offered as its representatives.

A further key element of initiatives such as neighbourhood watch, is recognition that community involvement is not merely preferable, but an essential element of crime control. It features in research in the United States (Greenwood and Chaiken 1977; Reiss 1971) and Britain (Bottomley and Coleman 1981; Mawby 1979) on the crucial role of the public in reporting crimes to the police and aiding the detection process. Indeed in the United States many victim services were a response to an appreciation that the criminal justice system depended on witness co-operation, for example, in agreeing to appear in court (Bolin 1980; Lowenberg 1981; MacDonald 1976; Schneider and Schneider 1981). It also emerged in the work of town planners and architects, where appreciation of the public as 'the eyes of the street' (Jacobs 1969) became subsumed into wider theories of situational crime prevention, with environment design a means by which – allegedly – citizen involvement could be enhanced (Mayhew et al. 1979; Newman 1972, 1976). It is equally evidenced in research showing the limits to preventative policing and the extent to which policing levels would have to be increased to effect any decrease in crime (Burrows et al. 1979).

Community participation in the criminal justice system is thus perceived as desirable in a number of ways from a variety of perspectives. However, community participation means different things to different people, not only in terms of levels of participation, but also in terms of the characteristics of those from the community who volunteer and the structure whereby such involvement is channelled and controlled. What precisely is meant by community involvement is thus debatable. In Chapter 2, we move on to consider the voluntary sector as one means of such involvement, and look to distinctions within the voluntary sector which allow us to identify different forms of participation in the criminal justice system.

2

THE ROLE OF THE VOLUNTARY SECTOR IN CONTEMPORARY BRITAIN

THE VOLUNTARY SECTOR AND THE MIXED ECONOMY

The Wolfenden (1978) Committee identified three alternatives to state-run services: the informal system of social helping, the voluntary system, and the commercial system. Combined, these comprise 'the mixed economy of welfare', allegedly preferable to state monopolization according to Wolfenden, because it widens range and choice of services.

The last decade has, however, seen a dramatic change of emphasis. Whereas Wolfenden was concerned to preserve a role for non-state services after a post-war period of unprecedented rises in welfare expenditure, an increased role for the mixed economy is now well-established government policy, as we noted in Chapter 1. In this context, there are some advantages to the government in blurring the lines between these non-state alternatives (Mawby 1989). However, it is also evident that such lines are already somewhat unclear. Thus, whilst we shall here focus on the voluntary sector, it is useful to start by distinguishing between this and the informal and commercial systems. If we subdivide the voluntary sector into *voluntary organization* and *volunteers*, the point is easily made.

What, for example, is a voluntary organization? While we probably all 'know' what we mean when we talk of a voluntary body, rigorous definitions are illusive. Academics have solved – or perhaps avoided – the issue by specifying ideal types (Brenton 1985; Hatch 1980; Johnson 1981). Accordingly, voluntary bodies tend to conform on five criteria:

1 They are initiated independently of the State.
2 They are not controlled or directed by the State, for example, regarding decisions on services or clients.

3 They are not financed exclusively by the State.
4 They are non-profitmaking (or at least non-profit *distributing*).
5 Acceptance of clients is not based on prior membership or an ability to pay.

This ideal type however illustrates a number of problems (Mawby 1989) of which two are worth noting here. First, private agencies are not distinctive from voluntary bodies on the first three criteria, and in the case of many – BUPA and most private schools, for example – not on the fourth either. This is accentuated where, on the fifth criterion, clients do not 'choose' the service, as is common within the criminal justice system. Second, where voluntary bodies do not conform to all five criteria, how different should they be to warrant exclusion? Thus, the National Association for the Care and Resettlement of Offenders (NACRO) was initiated with Home Office support and receives considerable government funding, but still tends to be seen as a voluntary body. Similarly, a number of agencies like hostels for ex-prisoners, the single homeless or drug-users are funded almost exclusively by the State, and yet are seen as a distinct subcategory of voluntary 'special agencies' (Hatch 1980).

As far as voluntary organizations are concerned then, there is a degree of overlap between these and both state and private services. The situation with regard to volunteers is less ambiguous, although volunteers may be deployed within both state and voluntary bodies, and indeed within the private sector as well. However, at least two problems of definition do sometimes arise. First, given discussions over the desirability or otherwise of training volunteers and the extent to which volunteers should receive expenses or honoraria, in some cases volunteering may blur into the use of (poorly) paid auxiliaries or 'reserves'. Second, as illustrated in research which has attempted to analyse volunteering using a household sample (Central Statistical Office 1986), the barrier between the informal system of helping and voluntary work is sometimes wafer thin. The respondent who takes time to deliver meals on wheels to the elderly in the area is a volunteer; the respondent who daily cooks meals for one elderly neighbour is a 'good neighbour'. The respondent who is on call to counsel crime victims is a victim-support volunteer; the respondent who runs to help a passer-by who is being attacked is a 'good Samaritan'.

The point to stress here is that analysis of the voluntary sector cannot assume that it is either a discrete or a problem-free entity. A further issue develops from this; namely, that within the voluntary sector there is considerable diversity. To further illustrate this, the following two sections focus on voluntary organizations and volunteers, as we attempt to develop typologies for each.

A TYPOLOGY OF VOLUNTARY ORGANIZATIONS

Hatch (1980) has provided a useful dichotomy. He first subdivided organizations according to whether the work is carried out by volunteers or paid staff. For the former, he then distinguished between those which serve their own members (self-help groups or 'mutual aid associations') and those providing a service for others ('volunteer organizations'). For organizations dependent upon paid staff, he considered source of funding, distinguishing between those which were largely dependent on government grants (termed 'special agencies') and those which depended on donations and fees, which he called 'funded charities'. Using examples from the criminal justice system, we can thus distinguish:

1 mutual aid associations: neighbourhood watch, PROP, Alcoholics Anonymous (AA), Narcotics Anonymous (NA), and recent self-help groups formed to provide support for families of drug-users (Donoghoe et al. 1987).
2 volunteer organizations: rape crisis centres, women's aid refuges, victim-support schemes, Radical Alternatives to Prison (RAP), and the Howard League.
3 special agencies: hostels for ex-prisoners, single homeless, etc.
4 funded charities: NSPCC.

Hatch's model provides a useful basis for distinguishing between different voluntary bodies operating within the welfare and criminal justice systems, but it also suffers from a number of weaknesses. For example, it does not distinguish between agencies providing a direct service for clients and pressure groups; and organizations such as rape crisis centres and victim support, which are very different in many respects (Mawby and Gill 1987), fall within the same category. Conversely, agencies – such as victim support – may evidence features of different categories.

The overall problem with a typology such as this is where diversity foils attempts to compartmentalize. Let us take three slightly different examples as illustration. First, in many respects rape crisis centres and women's refuges, in Britain at least, are similar in philosophy to 'mutual aid associations' but since most helpers have not been subjected to rape or spouse abuse they have been categorized here as 'volunteer organizations'. Second, many agencies incorporate features of different categories – most victim support schemes, for example, depend on volunteers but increasingly employ paid staff (see Chapter 5) and are becoming more dependent on state funding. Finally, some organizations may vary according to the different types of service they provide. For example, overall the National Children's Homes would be considered a 'funded charity'; but in the context of its work with juvenile delinquents and at-risk children it depends on state funds and in this respect might almost be seen as a 'special agency'.

Elsewhere, therefore, we have developed an alternative form of typology to distinguish different victim services in Britain and North America (Mawby and Gill 1987) by classifying agencies on four separate – but not exclusive – dimensions:

1 the relationship between the voluntary agency and state services.
2 source of funding.
3 goals.
4 the relationship between helper and helped.

FIGURE 2.1   Classification of voluntary agencies within the criminal justice system

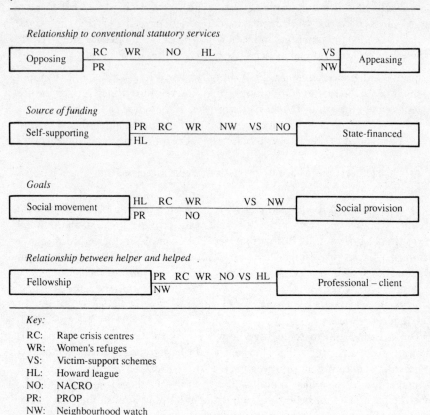

Relationship to conventional statutory services

| Opposing | RC   WR   NO   HL | VS | Appeasing |
| | PR | NW | |

Source of funding

| Self-supporting | PR RC WR   NW VS NO | State-financed |
| | HL | |

Goals

| Social movement | HL RC WR   VS NW | Social provision |
| | PR   NO | |

Relationship between helper and helped .

| Fellowship | PR RC WR NO VS HL | Professional – client |
| | NW | |

Key:

RC: Rape crisis centres
WR: Women's refuges
VS: Victim-support schemes
HL: Howard league
NO: NACRO
PR: PROP
NW: Neighbourhood watch

In Figure 2.1 we have used these to locate a number of the voluntary agencies already cited. Taking first the relationship between the voluntary agency and state services, we find at one extreme those like neighbourhood watch and victim support which work in close co-operation with one or more state service; at the other rape crisis centres, PROP and many women's refuges which are largely conceived as a fundamental critique of state agencies. While in Britain the latter examples tend to be located politically to the left, this is not necessarily so, even with a right-wing government. Thus in the United States, Mothers Against Drunk Driving (MADD) is 'oppositional' but, in advocating more severe sentencing practices, scarcely left-wing. Similarly, the Guardian Angels, 'exported' to Britain in 1988–9, contrast with neighbourhood watch in having more problematic relationships with the police but appear to be politically to the right.

The second dimension, source of funding, is not surprisingly closely related to the former, since as we shall note below funding rarely travels without strings. Governments may thus be more willing to fund agencies whose values they espouse. Take the attitude of the Conservative government towards the funding policy of the Labour-controlled Greater London Council (GLC), for example:

> The vision underpinning the Labour GLC's massive promotion of voluntarism – embracing as it did black groups, lesbian and gay groups, feminist groups and peace groups, in addition to 'mainstream' voluntary organizations providing services for the elderly, disabled, etc. – was clearly at odds with the Tory vision of voluntarism; though 'worthwhile' voluntary effort, Jenkin promised, would have nothing to fear from the GLC abolition.
>
> (Sheard 1986: 31)

The link between political acceptability and funding viability is a strong one. As we have noted elsewhere (Mawby and Gill 1987), it is illustrative of the rather different development of rape crisis centres and women's refuges in Britain and the United States. Nevertheless, clearly many agencies which enjoy good relationships with statutory bodies or central or local government are not dependent on them for funds, and others which do receive government financial support can be critical of their benefactors. For example, the Howard League, while relatively self-supporting, enjoys good relations with the Home Office (Ryan 1978) and NACRO, although dependent on state finance, has maintained a degree of political independence.

The third dimensions, goals, relates to the distinction made by Pahl (1979) between social movement and social provision goals. Pressure groups, like PROP and the Howard League, fall at the social movement end of the continuum; neighbourhood watch is almost exclusively service based. Somewhere between, rape crisis centres have provided services for rape victims while prioritizing political and educational goals, and refuges have combined welfare and political goals. NACRO, which is primarily a pressure group, has incorporated a number of preventive and diversionary projects, and victim support, principally a service agency, although far less politically active than its North American equivalents (Mawby and Gill 1987), does attempt to influence governments *vis-à-vis* explicitly victim-related policies (see for example House of Commons 1984; Ralphs 1988).

The final dimension refers to the relationship between helper and helped. Here, neighbourhood watch – by definition – and PROP, by design, exemplify self-help organizations, in this respect distinguishing the former from the Guardian Angels and the latter from RAP and the Howard League. As already noted, rape crisis centres and women's refuges, although they are not commonly run by former victims, usually prioritize a philosophy of sisterhood whereby the barriers between helper and helped are minimized and are thus distinctly different from victim support.

We would not wish to pretend that these four dimensions allow a comprehensive analysis of voluntary agencies, but they at least illustrate the diversity of voluntary bodies, the more so when we consider that, for example, local women's refuges (Gill 1986a) or rape crisis centres (Blair 1985) may vary from one another on these issues. Moreover, they provide a base from which we shall subsequently evaluate voluntary-sector provision. At this point, however, we wish to consider volunteers in more detail and attempt an equivalent typology.

A TYPOLOGY OF VOLUNTEERS

As already noted, distinctions are sometimes made in the literature according to whether or not volunteers are trained, the availability and level of expenses, and the extent to which volunteering is an informal arrangement or a more long-term commitment to an organization, commonly a voluntary agency or state service. However, these themes are rarely given much attention, and indeed much of the emphasis has been on treating 'volunteers' as a homogeneous category.

True, a great deal of discussion has centred on the question, 'who volunteers?' Variations in age, social class, gender, etc., are pinpointed. Nevertheless, even in this respect differences are often minimized and most attention paid to the 'typical volunteer', identified by Aves (1969) and since as middle aged, middle class, married and female. In marked contrast, as we shall argue later, not only may volunteers differ according to the nature of the agency and service involved, but it is also presumptive to assume that people choose to do voluntary work in general, rather than home in on a specific agency or activity.

Here we wish to draw attention to six dimensions on which volunteers and the work they do may be distinguished on a structural level: status, power, role, intra-agency specialism, work programme and helper/-helped relationship. The last of these is equivalent to that described in our agency typology, except that one might address *actual* relationships rather than agency *ideals*, and we shall not consider it further here.

In Figure 2.2 we have used the other five dimensions and illustrated them by taking examples of volunteers working with three of the voluntary agencies cited in the previous section, plus five additional groups of volunteers: magistrates, prison Boards of Visitors, the Parole Board, the special constabulary and probation volunteers. As in the previous section, we shall consider each dimension in turn, drawing on these eight examples.

Considering status first, we here mean the *ease* with which one can become a volunteer with a particular agency. What is the more decisive – *choosing* to volunteer or being successfully *selected*? Clearly, very few agencies accept everyone who volunteers. Even agencies which find it difficult to attract volunteers may opt to fall short of target rather than recruit volunteers felt to be unsuitable. Alternatively, volunteers may be graded (overtly or covertly) with some assigned no more than basic tasks, and volunteer bureaux may act as gatekeepers whereby volunteers are filtered to agencies which will consider them acceptable. However, some volunteer statuses have considerable prestige attached to them, and membership is the result of either some form of election (as in the case of parent governors in schools) or selected by an élite.

FIGURE 2.2   Classification of volunteers within the criminal justice system

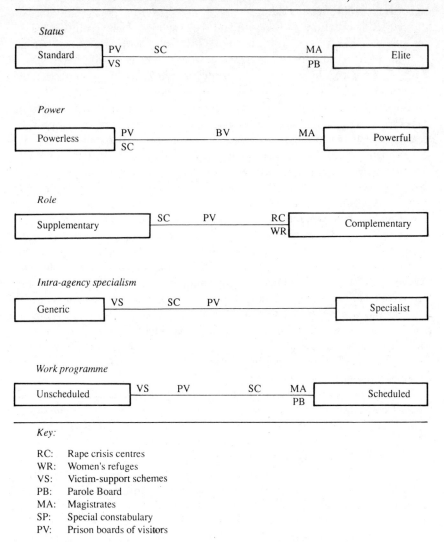

Key:

RC: Rape crisis centres
WR: Women's refuges
VS: Victim-support schemes
PB: Parole Board
MA: Magistrates
SP: Special constabulary
PV: Prison boards of visitors

For the magistracy, the Parole Board, or prison boards of governors equally, members of the public are 'chosen'; individual choice is only important in so far as the status of the 'calling' makes becoming, say, a magistrate, highly desirable. Indeed magistrates may be considered the élite apex to the volunteer pyramid for the criminal justice system. On the other hand, it is considerably easier to gain entrance to voluntary work with, for example, the probation service or victim support. Finally, with regard to the special constabulary, as we shall illustrate in Chapter 4, although individual decision making is important, agency screening and the length of the training period instil in volunteers the feeling that only a select minority are acceptable.

The second criterion, power, relates to the extent to which volunteers are able to influence the agency, its priorities, goals and methods (rather than the individual responsibility incumbent on the volunteer role). Two general tendencies emerge. First, where the agency is dominated by volunteers rather than professionals, one might expect volunteer power to be greater. Thus the special constabulary and probation volunteers fall to the left of the continuum, rape crisis centres and women's refuges to the right. Victim support lies somewhere between, with volunteer involvement perhaps muted by paid co-ordinators and management committees (Maguire and Corbett 1987). Second, where volunteers form an élite, one might anticipate power to be correspondingly great. However, while this is true of the magistracy, who have maintained some autonomy in sentencing decisions even against the wishes of government, élite volunteers may be relatively impotent where they are dependent upon paid employees for access and wider co-operation, as Maguire and Vagg (1984) have clearly illustrated in the case of prison boards of visitors.

The third dimension, role, relates to the distinction made by Holme and Maizels (1978) between complementary and supplementary services. We may see volunteers, on the one hand, involved in work which complements that of paid employees by providing an additional dimension, perhaps because of specialist expertise or just through their status as outsiders or ordinary members of the community. On the other hand, volunteers may supplement the work of paid employees by providing 'more of the same', or perhaps more of the more basic or mundane aspects of 'the same'.

If the examples already chosen are considered more fully, it seems clear that the special constabulary falls towards the supplementary end of the continuum, whilst radical alternatives to state services like rape crisis centres and women's refuges are at the other extreme.

The fourth criterion, intra-agency specialization, is another aspect of role, namely the extent to which the volunteer is involved (and perhaps recruited) as a specialist or to provide a more generic service. In this respect, most of the agencies used as examples tend to recruit and use volunteers in a generic context. Indeed, we might find differences most notable over time or between branches rather than on an organizational level. Thus, as we shall note in the following chapters, a few police forces may now recruit specials specifically for neighbourhood-watch schemes and many probation services commonly recruit volunteers for a particular task when it arises. Similarly, victim-support schemes may in the future follow this route as they begin to provide more specialist services in court or for victims of more serious crimes.

Finally, we might distinguish volunteers according to work programme, the timing of their voluntary work. At the one extreme lie agencies and volunteers where there is a relatively structured timetable, with one's voluntary work scheduled well in advance. Boards of visitors, the Parole Board, magistrates and special constables can be categorized at this extreme. At the other, due to the nature of the work, victim support tends to call on its volunteers at short notice and the amount of voluntary work done may fluctuate quite markedly. Somewhere between, probation volunteers may have their work structured in some respect but this will vary, according to the demands made by particular clients and the precise work carried out. On the other hand, women's refuges and rape crisis centres are likely to be relatively unstructured in their use of volunteers due to the informal nature of the agencies.

Viewed in this light, then, the work carried out by volunteers may vary enormously in its meaning and context. It may be carried out by an élite, with considerable say in how the agency operates, where the service provided is complementary to that of paid employees, where work schedules are structured, and where there is a degree of specialization. On the other hand, volunteers may be lacking in status or influence, providing a generic and supplementary service on an episodic basis. Our purposes in drawing out these distinctions are twofold. First, they provide a framework within which specific examples taken in Chapters 3–5 can be considered. Secondly, they provide a basis for our understanding of volunteer motivation and commitment, to which we shall return and which we shall assess from the perspective of the volunteer (Chapter 6) and the agency (Chapter 7). Here, however, we wish to continue on this more general level and raise a series of rather different issues by reviewing the alleged advantages and disadvantages of using volunteers and voluntary agencies.

THE BENEFITS OF VOLUNTARISM

As we have stressed elsewhere (Mawby and Gill 1987), much of the work on volunteering and voluntary agencies has been carried out by its disciples; not surprisingly, then, a number of claims have been made with regard to its benefits. At least seven are mentioned, some of which apply more readily to volunteers, some to agencies.

The first refers to the fact that the provision and variety of services are extended. The former is self-evident, unless voluntary work is merely a direct replacement for some other form of service. However, *variety* is only increased if the service provided through voluntary work is distinctly different from that provided by paid staff or state agencies, the distinction between supplementary and complementary services noted above. Thus, variety of services is only increased where the agency consciously plans a service which is distinctive and if the service could not have been provided by a statutory agency and/or paid staff. Unfortunately, in much of the literature this argument is settled through the unsubstantiated claim that voluntary agencies are 'naturally' preferable to state-run, impersonal bureaucracies, or correspondingly that volunteers in giving their time and services willingly are superior to paid staff.

A second advantage closely associated with this is that this extended provision leads to an overall improvement in the quality of the service; competitors are kept on their toes (Wolfenden 1978). This is often referred to with respect to voluntary bodies, but can also apply to volunteers, if paid staff are provoked to increased commitment by the enthusiasm and vigour of volunteers! Again, the argument is inconclusive; certainly an increased variety of services may improve consumer choice and overall efficiency, but why an increase in the types of service *providers* should do so is more questionable.

A third argument in favour of the voluntary sector, which is a specific example of the above, centres on the voluntary sector as pioneers. As Hugh Mellor (1985: 11) claims in enthusiastic advocacy of voluntary agencies:

> Because of its independence, and often because of its relative smallness of scale, the voluntary body is able to experiment, by doing old things in new ways, or trying out quite new services, and in so doing so take the risks which might be more difficult for a large and essentially more bureaucratic state concern.

Whilst it is clearly false to assume that new approaches to old problems are developed exclusively within the voluntary sector, it is equally true that voluntary agencies *have* been trailblazers (Brenton 1985) and statutory agencies have often found it convenient to use volunteers to address new issues (or old issues in new ways). Indeed many of the welfare services we have today emerged from voluntary initiatives. In the context of the criminal justice system, for example, as we noted in Chapter 1, the probation service in England and Wales was born of the initiative of the London police-court missionaries, and in the United States a Boston cobbler, John Augustus, is accepted as the first (volunteer) probation officer. More recently, in Britain and elsewhere, initiatives to provide services for victims of rape, domestic violence and other crimes, have been taken against a blackcloth of apathy from many statutory agencies. Again, within the statutory sector, the probation service has often used volunteers to provide new services – for defendants in court or for prisoners' wives, for example.

A fourth, and rather different alleged advantage of the voluntary sector relates to its role in pressure-group activities. The claim is made, with some justification, that voluntary bodies, being independent, can more readily attack government policies and the practices of statutory bodies. Again this clearly occurs, as illustrated in the examples given above, with regard to social-movement goals. Nevertheless, two points must be stressed. On the one hand, statutory agencies, or interest groups within them, are scarcely muted where they feel the need to criticize government or agency policy – witness conflicts within the National Association of Probation Officers (NAPO) or the Police Federation, for example. On the other hand, voluntary agencies are not equal in their eagerness to put pressure on governments, as Ryan's (1978) comparison of the Howard League and RAP well illustrates.

This relates to a fifth alleged advantage: that the voluntary sector provides an *independent* voice. This might be true of voluntary organizations which are not reliant on state funding, but, as Wolfenden (1978) illustrated over a decade ago, that era is fast receding; increasingly voluntary bodies depend on governments to fund them and to that extent *may* tone down their criticisms. Since in general paid employees in the voluntary sector are less unionized than their equivalents in the state sector, one could indeed argue that their independent voice is *more* muted. A similar issue applies with regard to volunteers working in statutory agencies. Morris (1969), for example, argued that, since volunteers were not dependent upon income, they would be more willing to criticize malpractices than would paid employees. However, as we noted above, volunteers may be dependent on paid staff to the extent that their independence is restricted, and in some cases their commitment to the agency may be such that they are hardly to be regarded as independent (Gill 1987).

The question of independence is ultimately connected to a sixth issue, that of cost. Reliance on voluntary agencies is cheaper than using statutory services if they raise their funds independently of the state, or if they are more 'efficient' – that is to provide a similar service at lower cost. In this respect, there is little evidence that an escape from state bureaucracy cuts costs, except where employees are paid at lower rates, a point equally applicable to the private sector and contracting-out services. Use of volunteers – whether by statutory or voluntary agencies – is, of course, one obvious route to cheaper services – although the extent of savings may be offset by the time taken by paid staff to train, organize and supervise volunteers. There is also a restriction on the types of work volunteers can do, notably in the context of the criminal justice system where legal responsibilities are involved. For example, despite the pervasiveness of criticisms of social-worker involvement in non-accidental injury (NAI) cases, the idea that volunteers could – or would want to – take over is scarcely appealing!

The final claim made on behalf of the voluntary alternative is rather more amorphous. It relates to the societal function of voluntary helping as a mechanism for increasing social cohesion. It is perhaps best exemplified in Titmuss's (1971) comparative study of blood donorship, where he argued that creation of the right atmosphere, in which citizens freely donated their blood to help anonymous others, was an essential ingredient of the good society. By this criterion then, it is important for societies to allow citizens the opportunity to give voluntarily should they so wish.

This is persuasive, although practically impossible to test in any quantitative way. Overall though it appears that the claims made on behalf of the voluntary sector have some substance, but there is little evidence that such benefits are exclusive to that sector: provision and variety may be extended, quality improved, innovations made, etc., by statutory or indeed private agencies.

PROBLEMS WITH THE VOLUNTARY SECTOR

There are, moreover, a number of problems regarding dependence, particularly increased dependence, on the voluntary sector. Six are of particular significance:

the relationship between volunteers and paid employees, volunteer–client relationships, area inequalities, the reliability issue, problems associated with funding, and finally the question of balance.

The relationship between volunteers and paid employees attains significance where employees see their jobs, status or overtime as threatened by an increasing use of volunteers. Additionally, if volunteers are motivated by 'interesting' work, then employees may find their workloads shifting. The Barclay (1982) Report, for example, in advocating an expansion of volunteer use, envisaged social workers as operating in a more administrative or managerial capacity, less involved at the 'coal-face' of client contact. A similar suggestion was made by Bottoms and McWilliams (1979) regarding probation. In each case, any change might be expected to have profound implications for social workers' or probation officers' job satisfaction. If volunteers, and their roles within the organization, do not therefore meet with the approval of employees of the agency in question, we might predict that at the very least the use and usefulness of volunteers are likely to be undermined.

The second problem concerns the relationship between volunteer and client, which, in the context of the *quality* of relationship is often referred to as an advantage of volunteer use. That is, it is alleged, volunteers, as ordinary members of the public, avoid the bureaucracy and its associated stigma in being able to build up meaningful and unthreatening relationships with clients, and duty is replaced by caring as the basic principle to the relationship. There are, however, two problems here. First, as noted earlier in this chapter, the helper–helped relationship is a variable and differs markedly *within* the voluntary sector. Second, as accepted by proponents of voluntarism, volunteers tend to be drawn predominantly from the middle classes. There is then no reason to suppose that overall the helper–helped divide will be less, or its impact less stigmatic. Indeed, if employees in welfare agencies, as members of the semi-professions (Etzioni 1969), consist of a disproportionate number of those from lower social-class backgrounds it might be that the divide is *greater* between volunteers and clients. Be this as it may, the problem of achieving a representativeness, or a balance, among volunteers is a longstanding one.

A third issue, which is closely connected to this, refers to ecological imbalance, best exemplified by Hatch and Mocroft (1977) in their research for Wolfenden (1978). In analysing data for major voluntary organizations in urban areas across the country, they found considerable variations with agencies best represented in southern, 'cathedral city' environments and least in northern industrial cities where unemployment and other levels of need were greatest. A similar picture emerges from our own research on volunteers (Mawby and Gill 1987; see also Chapter 3–5) and, as noted in Chapter 1, was also recognized as a problem by governments of the past. That is, where resources are dependent upon individual motivation and choice, there is no guarantee that these will adequately meet need; in areas where needs are greatest, voluntary agencies and volunteers may be thinly stretched. Alternatively, where needs are least there may be a surplus of volunteers. This is not to deny considerable geographical variation in the availability of statutory services. However, given the political will, it would appear that such differences can be minimized where resources can be reallocated between areas; the opportunity to 'bus' volunteers from one area to another is more limited!

Allied to the issue of ecological imbalance, and a fourth issue, is the unreliability of some volunteers. This does appear to be rather more true at the level of the individual as opposed to the organizations, although even on this level the point retains its value. It is a comment frequently mentioned by professionals, certainly to us in our research, and is perhaps an inevitable consequence of the nature of voluntary activity.

A fifth issue, and one of primary concern at the present time is the problems associated with state funding. As we have seen there are a number of facets to this point. A particular problem is the extent to which the provision of funds contaminates agencies, threatening a volunteer group's independence. The point is well made by Paul Lewis (1988):

> The voluntary sector can only be creative and critical if it is financially independent. It is less and less so. Central government support has changed from long-term general funding to short-term task-orientated projects where staff are too busy doing their immediate jobs, and too nervous of where next year's salary is coming from, to criticize their pay master.

Reliance on state funds has a further worry; that is where the need to seem efficient, to demonstrate one is providing a necessary and valued service, takes priority over *actual* efficiency and effectiveness. In Plymouth, for example, Blacher's (1989) evaluation of a local nightshelter for single homeless problem drinkers – which would have been included under Hatch's (1980) definition of a 'special agency' – shows that it continued to receive central-government funding, despite a poor quality of service provision, but also directed considerable efforts to demonstrating its usefulness by ensuring a reasonable level of occupancy whether or not it was the most appropriate accommodation for many of its clientele. Again, we would not wish to suggest that statutory agencies are as accountable in practice as they are in theory. However, it does appear to us that potential for permanency of funding and adequate accountability is greater for the public sector and weaker for the voluntary sector, especially where, as is commonly the case, within the criminal justice system, control by consumer choice is inoperative.

A final, and sixth issue, we mention with some irony, since it concerns the problems of a thriving voluntary sector if it is used to curtail state commitment to welfare services. This is, of course, a political issue and, for some, such an emphasis would be desirable. The problem is one of degree. As we have noted elsewhere (Mawby and Gill 1987) and will reiterate later, we support and in many cases prefer some services to be delivered voluntarily, including some essential services such as those for crime victims. However, we do have reservations about developments elsewhere. For example, Gillian Davies, as secretary to the trustees of the Allen Lane Foundation and chairperson of the Charitable Trusts Administrators Groups, was reported in the *Guardian* (14 September 1988) to have said:

> We're getting applications from quasi-medical groups for research money; from colleges of further education who want support for extra curricular activities, trips and equipment; from health authorities for psychiatric funding or speech therapists; from London boroughs wanting money for carers; from social services departments for help with individual hardship cases; from hospitals wanting funding for children's units; from employment schemes and from universities wanting help not just with their actual research but with the administration of it as well.

This, not surprisingly, led to protests from charities. In practice it is difficult to delineate appropriate or preferable boundaries for voluntary and statutory influence. However, it appears to us that on a very basic level, if the pioneering role of the voluntary sector or of charities specifically is threatened by the expectation they will fill gaps caused by a purposive curtailment of state provision, then the pendulum has swung too far.[1]

We have not intended our discussion to be exhaustive. Rather, it is important to point to just some of the main advantages and disadvantages of the voluntary sector and volunteers. In particular, it needs to be stressed that the relevance of each of these points will vary from time to time and from organization to organization. As such we shall consider them in more detail *vis-à-vis* specific agencies. At this point it appears appropriate to detail the criminal justice agencies which form the focus of the following chapters.

PROBATION, POLICE AND VICTIM SUPPORT

While, up till now, we have discussed the role of voluntary agencies and volunteers in general within the criminal justice system, the following chapters focus on three specific examples: probation volunteers,[2] police special constables and victim-support schemes. When we initially considered a project on the role of volunteers, we decided on a comparative study of their use in different agencies for a number of reasons. Principal amongst them was a concern that much research on volunteers has been at one or other of the extremes. That is, on the one hand, some studies have looked at volunteers working with a vast range of agencies or publics, such that differences between specific ones become submerged; on the other hand, much research has concentrated on volunteers in one agency, or working with one client group, without consideration of the distinctiveness of the situation. In contrast, we wished to be able to make more direct comparisons. We then chose the three main targets for our study according to three criteria.

First, was a wish to compare the use of volunteers in statutory agencies (probation, police) with an agency in the voluntary sector (victim support). Second, it seemed useful to compare agencies with different traditions in the deployment of volunteers. The special constables have been a feature of police forces almost since their inception; use of volunteers in probation has become a more significant issue in the last twenty-five years; and victim support is a comparatively recent development. Finally, and most important from a theoretical perspective, we wished to contrast situations where the ideological appeal of voluntary work might differ appreciably. The special constabulary is a disciplined organization evidenced by the wearing of uniforms, and markedly different from either probation or victim-support volunteers. Similarly these latter two groups are associated with one-to-one welfare work to an extent to which police work is not. Indeed, we originally hypothesized that those volunteering to help the probation service would be essentially volunteering to help *offenders*, victim support would attract those concerned with the needs of *victims*, and the police would appeal to those who saw the less tangible needs of the *community vis-à-vis* the crime problem. We thus wished to address not only the question of why some people become volunteers, but also why they volunteer for a specific type of activity with a specific type of agency.

In concentrating on the three agencies, we have started with a historical introduction. From this, we have moved on to review the international scene. This is, of course, dominated by material from North America, although there is a growing literature on Western Europe and Japan. We have then critically assessed the British data. For all three agencies, this involves a review of the published literature, including annual national statistics where appropriate, and we have also made full use of our contacts in different areas of the country, incorporating local discussion documents and in-house evaluations. For probation services we have also summarized the results of a short questionnaire we sent to all services in England and Wales in 1985, to which we received 43 replies.

Much of the wider literature is then discussed in the context of our more local research, which we conducted in Devon and Cornwall between 1983 and 1986. This involved five principal research strategies. First, we engaged in informal discussions with volunteers and those responsible for their co-ordination, including observation of management meetings, volunteer meetings and conferences, training sessions, and participation in a range of informal activities.

Second, we carried out analysis of the records kept by the three agencies on their voluntary workers. This covered all accredited probation volunteers in the two counties ($n = 219$), a sample of one-third of all registered police specials ($n = 250$), and all victim-support volunteers working in 12^3 schemes in Devon and Cornwall ($n = 107$). Third, using these as a sampling frame, a random sample was drawn for each agency, ensuring regional representation. Non-response for each agency was minimal, and extensive interviews were conducted with 58 probation volunteers, 51 police specials and 55 victim-support volunteers.

Fourth, we arranged with the police and probation services that all volunteers resigning during the research period would be automatically sent a short questionnaire aimed at eliciting personal details, reasons for their leaving, and views of the agency and voluntary work carried out. The small numbers of replies received from both police ($N = 24$) and probation ($N = 19$) 'resigned volunteers' limit any conclusions to be drawn from this aspect of the research, both none the less allow us to include an additional dimension.

Finally, we sent a postal questionnaire to all probation officers in Devon and Cornwall and a random sample of police officers, in order to elicit their experience of, and views on, both volunteers within their own agencies and victim support. Not unexpectedly, the response rate to these was somewhat lower than for the personal interviews, at 49 per cent and 65 per cent respectively, but completed questionnaires were received from 71 probation officers and 179 police officers.

Clearly, caution must be used in interpreting these findings. Although we have described them in the context of other studies, they are local, and as such may be representative of more rural areas, rather than the country as a whole. Nevertheless, given that areas such as the South-west are widely regarded as potentially fruitful sources for volunteers, it can be argued that the use of volunteers might be less problematic than elsewhere, and therefore a worthwhile environment in which to test out various ideas. Moreover, while we might not expect, say, probation volunteers in Devon and Cornwall to hold identical views to those in a more metropolitan area, we might justifiably argue that differences between probation volunteers and volunteers in other agencies might be suitably reflected elsewhere. This is, indeed, the foundation stone to comparative analysis of any sort.

One final point needs to be stressed regarding our own research. We have not considered consumers' perspectives of the value of volunteers compared with other helpers. Clearly this is an omission, and one which cannot unfortunately be rectified by reference to other studies. In the UK, for example, Maguire and Corbett's (1987) evaluation of victim-support schemes is one of the few studies in any area of the criminal justice system to include interviews with consumers of voluntary effort. It must therefore be emphasized that, whilst we have considered in some detail the work of volunteers from the perspectives of the agency, full-time employees, and volunteers themselves, the impact of voluntary work on those at whom the help is directed is less evident and requires closer consideration in future research.

OUTLINE

Having considered the role of the voluntary sector within the criminal justice system in general terms, the following chapters focus on three particular agencies – probation, police and victim support. For each we have adopted a similar format: a historical introduction, followed by a consideration of the current situation on an international and then national basis; then we focus on the South-west, describing the operation of voluntary work locally, who the volunteers are, professionals' perspectives, and the perspectives of the volunteers. In these three chapters many of the issues already raised will be reconsidered. However, data for the three agencies is more formally brought together in Chapters 6–7 when we assess the role of the voluntary sector, first from the point of view of the volunteers themselves and then in the context of the organizations within which they are situated.

3
VOLUNTEERS IN PROBATION

HISTORICAL INTRODUCTION

The origins of probation are commonly accepted to be found within the English common-law tradition as it was interpreted in England and the United States (United Nations 1951). In each country, efforts to contain the use of imprisonment in the nineteenth century led to practices within the courts whereby sentence might be deferred or suspended. From this arose the possibility that an offender might be bailed for a specified period under the charge of a responsible member of the community. John Augustus, a Boston (Massachusetts) cobbler, is alleged to be the first volunteer probation officer, after he agreed to stand bail for a man charged with drunken behaviour. Between 1841 and 1859 Augustus 'bailed on probation' almost 2,000 individuals. Following his death, a number of other volunteers carried on with probation in Boston, although these were gradually replaced by paid court officials, the first being in Boston in 1878 (United Nations 1951: 29–30).

In Britain, a similar process occurred, with probation supervision first being offered by police-court missionaries in London in the 1870s. Their first clients were drink-related offenders, but the 1887 Probation of First Offenders Act allowed them to extend the range of their clients to include more serious offences. Nevertheless, the probation role was a voluntary one until 1907 when the Probation of First Offenders Act incorporated a provision permitting local authorities to employ probation officers, a clause made compulsory by the 1925 Criminal Justice Act, and signalling the gradual erosion of the volunteer tradition (Jarvis 1971), in many ways paralleling trends in other areas of welfare.

Initiatives to rekindle volunteer interest were floated in the 1930s but thwarted by the Second World War (Stockdale 1985) and it was not until the 1960s, following the merger of the Probation Service with the After Care Service, that volunteers were significantly reintroduced to probation. The role and value of volunteers in this new arrangement were highlighted in the Reading (1967) Report, although there was a feeling among many probation officers that volunteers were a 'retrograde step' off the road towards professionalization of the service (Haxby 1978). There were, however, a number of local initiatives, especially regarding the use of volunteers in prison (Barr 1971). Thus, while in the late 1960s volunteer involvement was largely restricted to prison visiting and voluntary after-care support, by the mid-1970s volunteers were being used more widely and for a greater range of tasks (Holme and Maizels 1978; Leat and Rankin 1981; Younghusband 1978). Indeed, in their national survey at that time, Holme and Maizels (1978) concluded that probation services were more atuned to the potential for volunteer use than were social services departments. The latter have since been influenced by the recommendations of the Barclay (1982) Committee, and the Home Office (1984) response was to advocate a similarly expanded role for volunteers within probation. In a relatively short space of time then, volunteers appear to have regained a significant place within the probation service in England and Wales.

THE INTERNATIONAL SCENE

Although probation appears to have emerged from the English legal tradition, international comparisons can be made only with caution. The nature of the probation order, the range of work subsumed within probation departments, the typical client, and the working context of the probation officer vary over time and country (as well as *within* countries), and inevitably determine the boundaries within which volunteers operate. In the United States, for example, probation officers have relatively less involvement with aftercare provisions than in England and Wales and have higher caseloads (US Department of Justice 1988, 474–6),[1] and probation is more closely associated with intensive supervision (Byrne 1987; Erwin and Bennett 1987). In Japan probation officers work predominantly with juveniles and their work with adults mainly concerns prison aftercare (Hess 1970; Ministry of Justice 1982). That said, clearly some countries, among them Denmark, the Netherlands, Sweden and Japan, are heavily dependent upon volunteers (Baker and Baker 1966; Clifford 1976; Vizard 1988). In Sweden, for example, Becker and Hjellemo (1976: 104–5) reported an average of 92 clients and 48 volunteers for each probation officer,[2] and Hess (1970) described the Japanese system where the average field officer's main responsibilities surrounded co-ordinating the work of approximately 65 volunteers each working with about four clients!

The Japanese situation is particularly interesting, partly because Japan is a country in which low levels of welfare expenditure are to a certain extent compensated for by high levels of community and voluntary effort (Pinker 1986; see also Chapter 1). In addition, Japanese culture emphasizes obedience and loyalty (Nakane 1981). Thus probation volunteers, known as *hogoshis*, tend to be old, respectable, middle-class males whose relationship with their young clients approaches paternalistic authoritarianism (Hess 1970).

Despite examples such as these, much of the material on probation volunteers refers to the North American experience. In the United States, as in the United Kingdom, the role of volunteers tended to diminish as probation officers sought to attain professional status. The re-emergence of volunteers in the late 1960s in fact reflected concerns to improve agency–community relations and provide benefits to probationers, but was principally cost led: in some cases, for example, agencies were mandated by the legislature to use volunteers (Shields *et al.* 1983). The growing popularity of volunteers' usage is reflected in the extensiveness of the literature, although as Scioli and Cook (1976) observed some years ago, much of it is restricted to in-house publications.

A large amount of probation volunteer work in the United States (Scioli and Cook 1976) and Canada (James *et al.* 1977) tends to be with juveniles, especially on a one-to-one basis (Shields *et al.* 1983), although a wider range of services have been described in some areas (Schwartz 1971; Unkoviv and Davis 1969). However, Gandy's (1977) research in Canada is one of the few to dwell on volunteer work in an institutional setting. In one of the more detailed reviews of alternative work for probation volunteers, Shields *et al.* (1983) accept that one-to-one counselling, especially in juvenile programmes, is the most common manifestation. However, they also describe alternatives, including help with pre-sentence investigations (the equivalent of Social Enquiry Reports (SERs)), clerical work and courtroom assistance. They also provide examples of the use of volunteers as 'probation officer aids', carrying out a similar range of tasks to the probation officer, although they suggest that this is most appropriate for graduates seeking experience prior to a career in probation or allied work.

The North American literature also contains considerable information on the social characteristics of volunteers. To a certain extent, programmes have prioritized the need to recruit volunteers across a wide range of classes and ethnic groups, with some success, as Fo and O'Donnell (1974) illustrated for Hawaii. Moreover, as Eskridge and Carlson (1979: 187) stress:

An effort should be made to recruit volunteers with socio-economic backgrounds similar to the probationer population and a special effort made to become more responsive to the female probationer.

Nevertheless, Dowell's (1978: 358) conclusion that 'volunteers tended to be middle aged, female and middle class', confirmed by other researchers (Scheier 1970; Unkoviv and Davis 1969) sounds depressingly familiar, although some studies suggest a younger age profile (Gandy 1977; Horejsi 1971), possibly reflecting the incorporation of college students as volunteers in North America.

If this sounds familiar to a British audience, it is interesting to note at least one contrast in emphasis, with the importance of (quite extensive) training pro-grammes for volunteers taken for granted by researchers in both the United

States (Fo and O'Donnell 1974, 1975; Horejsi 1973; Howell 1972) and Canada (Mounsey 1973).

The issue of volunteer training, allied to the use of volunteers to cut costs, raises the question of volunteer–professional relationships. This is clearly a crucial issue in the effective use of volunteers (Ellenbogen and Digregorio 1975; Goddard and Jacobson 1967; Scheier 1970; Scheier and Goter 1969), and evidence of staff scepticism or direct hostility to the use of volunteers has been noted (Unkoviv and Davis 1969; Wood 1980). Nevertheless, as Gandy (1977) in particular found, volunteers tended to hold favourable attitudes of both the work and the professionals with whom they were involved, although they were somewhat critical of the ways in which they were being deployed. The author concluded:

Less than half the volunteers who stated they had special skills were actually using these skills in their work with inmates. There was no indication that an effort had been made to identify the special skills or to develop programmes designed to use them.

(Gandy 1977: 1)

How effectively are volunteers thus being used in North America? Although evaluation has been the main aim of much of the research on probation volunteers, as Scioli and Cooke (1976) correctly observed, in many cases the methodology is poor. Moreover, it is difficult to assess how far studies test out the use of volunteers in general, or more specific use of volunteers in quite distinctive programmes. Nevertheless, with some exceptions (Ellenbogen and Digregorio 1975) the conclusions of much of the research are at best mixed, at most pessimistic, and it generally appears that volunteer involvement is no more (but no less) effective in changing behaviour than conventional intervention (Dowell 1978; Eskridge and Carlson 1979; Fo and O'Donnell 1974, 1975; Poorkaj and Bockerman 1973; Scioli and Cook 1976).

Conclusions such as these may fuel attempts to scale down volunteer involvement. Alternatively, they may provoke concern that programmes should be managed more effectively. What is most significant about Wood's (1980) research in Ontario, for example, is the extent to which disorganized pro-grammes can breed widespread dissatisfaction amongst all those involved. Thus Mounsey (1973), in defending volunteer programmes, argues that the lack of conviction evident among staff using volunteers stems from a lack of clarity over the rationale behind volunteer involvement. He then tackles in turn many of the criticisms which have been raised by professionals and researchers and emphasizes the importance of training professionals to best utilize volunteers. He concludes:

While criticism of, and objections to, volunteers do have a basis they are often over stated. A more constructive approach would be to stress that these problems can be minimized by the skilful use of recruiting techniques, screening methods and clear role definitions. In addition, adequate orientation, support and careful volunteer supervision will do much to minimize some of the negative aspects and risks which are always associated with new programmes.

(Mounsey 1973: 57)

Bearing these points in mind, it is appropriate here to turn to a fuller consideration of British experiences of volunteers in probation.

THE NATIONAL PICTURE

Despite the fact that it is only comparatively recently that probation services have seen volunteer use as advantageous, Holme and Maizels (1978) found that by the mid-1970s officers more readily and more systematically deployed volunteers than did social workers. Thus 70 per cent of probation officers were then using volunteers and proportionally more of the rest – compared with social workers – had previously worked with volunteers. A similar picture emerges from national surveys of probation services conducted by the Volunteer Centre (Leat and Rankin 1981) in 1976 and 1980. In 1976 only 2 from 48 services that replied did not utilize volunteers; in 1980, all 44 services that replied did so, and over 5,000 volunteers were accredited at that time.

Such overall figures may be misleading, since the limited number of hours worked by volunteers, highlighted by Brenton (1985) is aggravated by findings that probation services are particularly guilty of under-using them (Stockdale 1985). A further problem emerges if one considers variation between services and areas of the country.

This is illustrated by responses to our own questionnaire, sent in 1985 to each service in England and Wales. In all 43 of the 56 services replied, a response rate of 77 per cent which is similar to that for the Volunteer Centre's earlier survey. All but one were currently using volunteers, the exception being the City of London Service which is unique in many respects. Of the rest, the number of accredited volunteers in 1984 ranged from 6 to 404 with a median of 84. According to our replies a minority of volunteers were not accredited,[3] principally those carrying out only basic tasks or those still undergoing training. Including those, the number of volunteers ranged from 16 to 458 with a median of 114.

Some degree of variation is to be expected, given differences in the size of different probation services. We therefore compared numbers according to population in the service's area and according to number of probation officers. Again there were marked variations. The number of accredited volunteers per 100,000 population ranged from 1.5 to 38.4 with a median of 11.0 and the ratio of accredited volunteers to probation officers ranged from 0.16 to 2.94 around a median of approximately one to one. Moreover, variations may also occur *within* probation services. For example, Murgatroyd (1987) shows that within Hereford and Worcester, a service with an overall high volunteer ratio, there were 3 volunteers per probation officer in the Redditch office but only 1.6 in the Worcester area.

Variations at office or service level may, of course, be a reflection of different sets of pressures. On the one hand, they may be indicative of ecological influences on volunteer recruitment, a point stressed on a general level by Wolfenden (1978) following Hatch and Mocroft (1977). On the other hand, they may be indicative of management attitudes towards volunteer use and the desirability of prioritizing recruitment. This is certainly the case within probation but also occurs in the context of other agencies which impinge upon the deployment of probation volunteers. For example, we found one prison where the governor had blocked the use of prison visitors.

What then of differences between probation services? Using a Pearson correlation, and allowing for variations in population in each probation service area, it was evident that probation staffing levels were higher in more densely populated areas where recorded offender rates and workloads were higher. This is scarcely surprising. However, in complete contrast, volunteer rates tended to be higher in areas with lower recorded offender rates and lower average workloads among probation officers. To illustrate this, we can divide responses to our questionnaire according to the amount of crime processed through the courts, controlling the population size. Of the 21 services with low crime rates by this measure, 15 (71 per cent) had more volunteers than probation officers; of the 22 with high rates, only 7 (32 per cent) had more volunteers.

This should not be taken as a denial of the impact of managerial policy on recruitment. As we shall show later with regard to our local study, officers committed to the use of volunteers were a primary prerequisite for effective volunteer deployment. This raises the question of the range of tasks carried out by volunteers.

Clearly the range is extensive, as numerous writers have indicated (Baillie 1967; Clarke 1977; Colver 1969; Jarvis 1980; Stockdale 1985), with involvement in 'individual befriending outside prison' and 'prison visiting', especially common (Leat and Rankin 1981), reflecting Barr's (1971) assertion that volunteers preferred to be involved in ongoing casework with clients. However, a majority of services also cited literacy schemes, prisoners' wives groups, other group work, intermediate-treatment programmes, day-centre work, transport, accommodation services and fund raising.

In our national survey, we asked services to rank the most common tasks from a list of four. The results are illustrated in Table 3.1.

Whilst the emphasis here tends to suggest somewhat traditional tasks – especially 'befriending' (see Holme and Maizels 1978), 'one-to-one' work – a number of replies indicated that this situation was changing. For example:

> Until a couple of years ago I would have placed 'Providing Transport' second – but teaching social skills and Literacy Schemes in Day Centres now involves a number of roles on a regular basis.   (PS16)

TABLE 3.1 Rank order of most common tasks
undertaken by volunteers

	Mean rank
Work with individual clients	1.1
Work with groups	2.1
Providing transport	3.0
Committee work	3.8

Work generally seems to be traditional, i.e. one-to-one befriending. There are some working in groups, day centres, wives' group activities and occasionally providing transport. One great development in X is a bus scheme, ferrying passengers to institutions regularly at weekends. The whole scheme is run by volunteers and they do a great job. (PS7)

In the statement of Local Objectives and Priorities, we have noted our lack of adequate provision for those sentenced to very short terms of imprisonment, i.e. few days to 10 months. A scheme has been established . . . so that clients locally should be followed through by the use of volunteers working especially with petty, inadequate offenders. (PS2)

Interestingly, this wide range of tasks provided by volunteers was recognized by some as having implications for the recruitment of volunteers. That is, it was sometimes advantageous to recruit for a specific project rather than fitting a 'generic' volunteer into a distinctive and relatively autonomous unit. For example:

It is important that volunteers are increasingly recruited and used for specific work rather than 'befriending'. (PS60)

Increasingly we recruit horses for courses – if we need someone to link up drug takers in the prison with local drug services, we recruit someone from that service – to help run an alcohol programme we look to Council on Alcoholism, as an interpreter to Colleges, for babysitting to sixth forms, to visit the lonely over 65-year-old pensioners in the Local Prison we look for someone retired, to help organize a marathon – someone from the army, to assist with a motor project – we find staff from the Helicopter base, for supporting single-parent families – we find suitably motivated housewife/parents, etc. (PS10)

How, then, are volunteers commonly recruited? We gave services a list of the five alternatives which have most commonly been cited in the literature (Aves 1969; Humble 1982; H. Jackson 1985; Morris 1969; Murgatroyd 1987), plus one 'other' category, and asked them to rank their use. As is clear from Table 3.2, three general patterns were evident from replies. First, the two most common

TABLE 3.2 Rank order of different methods used to recruit volunteers

	Mean rank
Recommended by other probation volunteers	2.3
General inquiry from public	2.5
Recommendations from probation officers	3.2
Through a volunteer bureau	3.5
Advertisements in media, etc.	4.0

means of recruitment were on the recommendations of another probation volunteer and via general inquiries. Second, and rather less common, were recommendations from probation officers and referrals from volunteer bureaux. Finally, the media were used less frequently. Interestingly, there was a slight variation in ranking according to the proportion of volunteers in the service. Areas with lower volunteer rates were likely to rate general inquiries as the most common method and volunteer recommendations second, the reversal of the pattern in higher volunteer rate areas.

Apart from the five methods listed, three additional sources were noted. First, a few probation services in the London area pointed out that their volunteers were recruited via SOVA.[4] Second, a number of services mentioned that they commonly recruited from among members of the public enquiring about a career in probation, who would be advised to gain experience first through voluntary work.[5] Third, a few services mentioned other agencies which recommended potential volunteers to them, such as social-services departments or the bench.

The question of recruitment, however, carries with it at least two further implications – that volunteers fulfil useful services and that more volunteers are needed. As already noted, this second issue has been challenged by Stockdale (1985) and indeed Hill (1981) found that as many as a quarter of respondents were not being used at the time of the research. This may reflect an 'oversupply' of volunteers; more likely it suggests poor management and an ambivalence about the desirability of expanding the role of volunteer, echoing the North American literature.

On this latter point, Holme and Maizels (1978) reported the generally favourable views of probation officers on experiences of using volunteers; 50 per cent saw advantages for their own workload and 35 per cent felt it had personally benefited clients. Moreover, half their sample also felt volunteers had 'something different and extra' to give (Holme and Maizels 1978: 103). However, whilst 45 per cent of probation officers said there were no disadvantages in deploying volunteers, others focused on problems associated with the amount of time and effort required of paid staff and the lack of skill and experience of volunteers.

In our own survey, we asked an open-ended question on the two greatest advantages of having volunteers. Replies were subsequently coded into four general categories. Of these, the least common, cited seven times, referred to the basic functions that volunteers could fulfil – providing transport, or in other ways taking the mundane tasks off the shoulders of probation officers. More commonly, 16 replies focused on the extra resources volunteers provided, allowing an increased level of contact with clients. The two most commonly expressed categories of replies, however, centred around the particular advantages of having non-professionals, ordinary members of the community, involved in the service. As many as 21, in fact, stressed these 'community' links. For example:

As local volunteers they may help to breakdown/reduce the stigma of being an offender living in the community. (PS39)

Volunteers provide an essential link with the community, and access to their own formal and informal networks. (PS43)

They bridge the gap between the service and the community. (PS46)

Ability to help client 'back into' the local community because of their own contacts and demonstration that the community cares. (PS16)

Closely allied to this were a series of answers which reflected a feeling that there were attributes which volunteers could bring to the service which, while distinct from the professional skills and relationships of the probation officer, were equally beneficial. These ranged from specific skills to commitment, enthusiasm and spontaneity, allowing for a qualitatively different helper–helped relationship. For example:

Increased befriending by people with a practical, non-professional approach allowing for a regular, reliable contact with a small number of clients. (PS47)

Often a more understanding and relaxed relationship between client and volunteer than is possible at an 'official' level. (PS40)

The benefit from expertise of volunteers such as life experience, particular skills, i.e. teaching numeracy, literacy, etc. (PS53)

As is clear from these examples, many of these categories inevitably overlap. What is important to stress, however, is the extent to which probation volunteers are seen by respondents not just as additional 'bodies', but as outsiders bringing to the service a range of benefits precisely *because* they are 'outsiders'. Three paragraphs attached to one questionnaire are an excellent illustration of an often repeated theme:

We should never use a volunteer primarily to save money – but they may be used to perform tasks which ideally the Service would like to undertake but realistically will never be able to find the money to do. Victim support schemes and a regular welfare-rights advice service are examples of this.

Volunteers are not an unpaid substitute for a Probation Officer or Assistant and it is important for management to be clear where lines are drawn, as confusion can occur in some settings (e.g. where it may seem to the layman that the volunteer is deputizing for a Probation Officer – whilst in reality he is releasing the Probation Officer to perform more skilled services by under-taking routine functions, e.g. in Court).

Volunteers bring many additional skills to service gained through life experience or because they are members of the local community rather than having the 'professional', 'social worker' authority label. The most important contribution of volunteers, therefore, is the added dimensions which they bring to the work of the Service.   (PS29)

On the surface, such glowing testimony begs the question of why volunteers are not more readily used. Additionally, though, it hints at some of the difficulties which arise in the recruitment and deployment of volunteers. These are reflected in responses to the next question, where we asked about the 'two greatest difficulties which arise from having volunteers in Probation'. In total 76 replies were coded, of which 51 could be categorized under one of four headings. Nine replies related to the characteristic of volunteers – for example, where unsuitable or unreliable volunteers were appointed, or where there was not an appropriate balance or mix of volunteers with different social characteristics (a problem the agencies could well address – see Chapter 7). A further seven replies focused on the problems of getting volunteers where and when they were needed. However, the two areas most commonly mentioned covered the costs engendered (17 replies) and the attitudes of probation officers (18 replies). In the former, respondents noted the costs incurred by volunteers due to the need for supervision, administration, support, training and travelling costs (see also Holme and Maizels 1978; Leat and Rankin 1981). Interestingly, such replies were most common from services with a higher proportion of volunteers. Answers relating to the attitudes of probation officers ranged from lack of enthusiasm to outright hostility engendered by wider political influences. For example:

Feeling among some Probation officers of erosion of professional status, substitution.   (PS27)

The present government has stressed the need for more voluntary effort and made available extensive funds for the development of volunteers. An increasing number of professionals are becoming suspicious of the possibility of volunteers substituting for tasks carried out by them at present.   (PS37)

Moreover, general feelings of mistrust and hostility among probation officers might, in a suitable environment, feed off the acceptance that the effective use of volunteers does take time and effort – that is, it is *not* a no-cost resource. Thus a number of replies linked the importance of organization and supervision with the ambivalence or hostility of many probation officers. For example, one respondent saw the problem as one of 'Convincing basic grade Probation officers that they *are* worth time and trouble' (PS43).

Our findings therefore reflect the body of scepticism, which as Stockdale (1985) discusses in detail, has real implications for the wider use of volunteers. Indeed, if the 1960s could be seen as an era of regeneration, and the 1970s as a period of hope and expansion, then the 1980s is very much the era of realism. The results of our national survey reflect the tenuous balance between enthusiastic support and wariness. Too often the notion that the probation service *ought* to involve volunteers has not been matched by planning and commitment in practice. What is clear is that the effective use of volunteers includes the need for adequate training, support and supervision.

USE OF VOLUNTEERS IN DEVON AND CORNWALL

The counties of Devon and Cornwall have separate probation services with their headquarters situated in Exeter and Truro respectively. At the time of our research in 1983–5, Devon had some 14.6 probation volunteers per 100,000 population, or 1.2 per officer; the corresponding figures for Cornwall were somewhat higher at 16.0 and 2.1 respectively. Both were thus somewhere above the national average.

The fact that probation volunteers are not spread evenly throughout the two counties is well illustrated by a consideration of rates (per 100,000 on the electoral register) for the sixteen parliamentary constituencies separately. These reveal the predominance of Exeter as a 'good volunteer country' in this respect (see also Hatch and Mocroft 1977) with a rate of 35.3 followed by Devon West and Torridge (30.2), with the three Plymouth constituencies at the other extreme with rates of between 10.4 and 13.6.[6]

Each probation service is organized on a team basis, with each team headed by a senior probation officer with responsibility for either a specific area or task, or both. Probation volunteers were usually attached to a team, although this was not always the case. For example, a volunteer could work simply with one officer, or – at the other extreme – with more than one team. Again, in some teams it would be the senior who was responsible for volunteer co-ordination, in many others this role was delegated to a main-grade officer, or auxiliary, usually in conjunction with a volunteer representative.

National data indicating the variety of tasks carried out by probation volunteers is replicated here. About half the volunteers we interviewed were involved in 'befriending', that is ongoing casework with a client, work emphasized in Ward's (1984) account of one area of Devon. This frequently, but by no means always, took the form of prison visiting. In contrast, many volunteers were involved in day centres, reflecting their recent growth within the service (James 1985) and an expanding market for volunteer activity. Indeed, at least one group was run exclusively by volunteers. Apart from day centres, other fields of organized activity were common. These included prisoners' wives, alcohol, literacy and football groups. Of the remainder, some were involved in specialist work; for example, one group of volunteers were attached to a divorce-court welfare team, and others dealt only with supervising community service orders. Some occupied their time providing transport facilities, ensuring that wives of prisoners were able to visit their husbands, or accused clients summoned to appear in court arrived on time. Two volunteers were private landladies, whose tenants were selected almost exclusively from probation-service clients. Their accreditation enabled them to claim travelling expenses, a facility technically not available to the unaccredited. Volunteers were then involved in many aspects of the work of the probation service.

This is not, however, the same as saying that volunteers were all actively involved! Here the results paint a dismal picture, with 41 per cent inactive at the time of the interview. For some, contact with the service had been severed in that, as far as they were concerned, they had resigned, although, having never submitted an official letter, and having never been asked to submit one, their names remained on record. Others were inactive because they were taking a rest from voluntary work, or because they were otherwise engaged.

Nevertheless, a major contributory factor to the high level of inactivity was the fact that there was a dearth of referrals available. One probation volunteer had never, one year after her accreditation, been approached by the probation service, suggesting that Riddick's (1984) experience was not an isolated case. Indeed, other volunteers to whom we spoke lamented their under-use at some time in the past, and only 41 per cent claimed they were doing the right amount at the time of the interview, with as many as 53 per cent wanting to increase their involvement.

Similarly, when later in the interview, respondents were asked whether they considered the probation service made full use of them, as many as 60 per cent felt they could be more widely used. Some typical comments included:

> The probation officers always seem to be very busy. The simple answer is no, because volunteers keep saying they have not got enough to do. The trouble is that you can enlist too many and keep them standing around. (PV 08)

> I would like to know the answer myself. They always say how busy they are, but we don't hear anything for months. They don't say anything. (PV 18)

The role of probation officers as work providers will be evaluated below. Here it is necessary to record that, at a time when volunteers perceived probation officers to be overworked, they were being overlooked as a potential source of help.

Of those who were active, just under a fifth were committed for less than two hours weekly, with slightly more than this undertaking between two–four hours. The remainder were involved in more (in one instance amounting to three full days each week at a day centre). Just as the hours allotted to voluntary work varied, so did the number of clients with whom they were engaged. Not surprisingly though, given the paucity of cases available, most were only involved with one or two clients. Of those who had been referred at least one client, contact with them tended to occur quite frequently. For 60 per cent it was at least weekly and for nearly a third of these it exceeded once a week.

Whilst various methods of matching volunteer to clients have been devised, little evidence exists on the type of people volunteers would prefer to visit. However, when asked about the preferred age and gender of clients, the majority of respondents replied that they were unconcerned. Nearly all of those who did express a preference, and all of the men who did, suggested someone of their own gender and possibly someone younger rather than older. With regard to gender, this corresponds with Barr's (1971) observation that probation officers' practices were to match male with male.

Overall there was very little evidence of conscious attempts to match the qualities and character of the volunteer with those of the client. There are perhaps two reasons for this. First, volunteers placed few limits on whom they would or would not visit. Indeed, when asked about the preferred age and gender of clients, the majority of respondents replied that they were unconcerned. Most of those who did express a preference, and all of the men who did, suggested someone of their own gender and possibly someone younger rather than older.

Second, and most importantly, was the low priority matching afforded by probation officers. Indeed, only two of our respondents had ever been asked by an officer what sort of work they would most like to do. Thus even matching the *task* was not common. In fact the allocation process frequently militated against effective matching, since officer(s) would often use volunteer meetings to state which cases were available and invite all in the volunteer group to make a claim.

Of course, it is far from obvious that volunteers would necessarily know that they had been 'matched'. However, observation at probation-volunteer meetings tended to confirm that it was a rare event. Occasionally, at meetings, particularly in discussion over cases, reference was made to a specific character-istic of the volunteer which helped in work with the client. On one occasion a (male) probation officer admitted that a (female) volunteer had succeeded in establishing a rapport with a client where he had failed 'partly because I was the wrong sex'. Often though it appeared that such advantages were gained incidentally. For example, one volunteer who had found herself helping the wife of a probationer, mentioned to us: 'It was important that I had children, in fact I have a daughter of the same age and this allowed me to help.'

Matching in general then was not perceived as an issue by officers or a problem by volunteers. The vast majority, well over three-quarters, had never refused a client but, for those who had, a lack of time at the point the request was made was frequently cited as the reason. Nevertheless, there were a few who refused a client because of some knowledge about the case. For example:

Because I know the family so well.   (PV 09)

Because it was somebody I know very well, not that I mind knowing somebody afterwards, it was very difficult beforehand.   (PV 36)

In a rather different context this raises important questions about the role of volunteers in helping their neighbours when one of the parties has been defined as criminal. Indeed, behind policies of care by the community, in whatever guise, rest assumptions that help will be provided indiscriminately. Since this is a central concern in the modern use of volunteers, we incorporated a number of questions to ascertain volunteers' views of its applicability to probation practice.

One potential danger of being a probation-service volunteer, and working with offenders, as Lacey (1963) found in his study, is the risk of victimization. During the course of the research a few examples were recounted to us. These varied from a threat of violence, to theft from a purse, to not repaying loans.[7] The volunteers did not consider them serious (even if they were annoying), and they were rare, but they did occur. Nevertheless, when asked, most volunteers were not opposed to working in their home area. Indeed, when we asked those who had not worked with clients locally how they would react if they were asked to do so, indicating their answer on a scale from 'very favourable' to 'very unfavourable', over a third were 'indifferent', but more were in favour than against. Moreover, the latter group tended to stress the debilitating effect this might have on the clients, rather than any adverse inconvenience to themselves.

Some volunteers took the notion of working locally a stage further. Indeed, 43 per cent had invited clients back to their home. Those who were more experienced (having been a probation volunteer for more than three years) were significantly more likely to have done so. On the other hand, inexperienced volunteers were more likely to state that having clients in their home had caused them problems (71 per cent of those with less than three years' service compared to only 19 per cent of those with more than three years' service).

But in all rather fewer cited problems than advantages, in some instances for both volunteer and client. For example:

He was a good plumber, and did my plumbing for me. Did a marvellous job so I gave him a plumb placement.   (PV 13)

We gave a job to the husband. He painted the outside of the house. It was wonderful.   (PV 18)

Nevertheless, of those who had not invited a client back to their home, most were opposed to the idea. The principal objection lay in complicating their relationship. Some claimed they would resent combining voluntary activity and home life which they preferred to see as separate. Interestingly, similar results were obtained in response to a question on whether or not they had ever given their home telephone numbers to clients. Despite the fact that probation officers generally advised against the practice, 64 per cent of volunteers answered in the affirmative. However, two-thirds of the remainder stated that they would never do so.

This would suggest a group of volunteers whose involvement was on a different level to others. The majority were not opposed to working with clients in their home area, and most did, or would, provide them with their telephone number and invite them back to their abode. To this extent the role of the community in looking after itself appears to be an idea which receives some welcome support. However, a caveat is necessary here in that a small but significant minority had been victimized by their clients, and so those who are particularly vulnerable (for example, those living alone) may have more to lose as a result of this type of in-depth involvement. Furthermore, a significant minority wished to see their voluntary work as separate from their immediate vicinity, and this should be borne in mind when advocating policies of care by the community, at least in a probation context.

However, whilst volunteers were committed to a wide variety of tasks with many clients, they throughout expressed disillusion at their under-use, against a background where officers lamented their heavy workloads. We shall return to this point in considering in more detail the views of probation officers and volunteers. Before doing so, however, we can briefly focus on the characteristics of the volunteers themselves, and their reasons for undertaking voluntary work.

PROBATION VOLUNTEERS

Who becomes a volunteer is a product of at least two processes: first, the application process, that is those who offer their services (an individual decision), and second, the selection process, considering which of the applicants is acceptable (an organizational decision). These two components frequently go unrecognized. It is often lamented that volunteers are atypical in terms of the public generally – and since they are unrepresentative, so the argument goes, their value is lessened. Yet little attention is focused on the role of the agency in determining who gets selected, and in particular in perpetuating that bias.

So how are volunteers recruited? We have already noted that, on a national level, probation services were most likely to rank recommendations by other volunteers as the most common source, followed by general inquiries and probation-officer recommendations. In the South-west over half our sample noted a probation source, although the role of probation officers rather than volunteers was emphasized. Such a finding parallels Murgatroyd's (1987) research in Hereford and Worcester and Barr's (1971) earlier work. Many volunteers we spoke to mentioned that they initially heard about voluntary work via a talk from a probation officer. Moreover, the word-of-mouth recruitment method, widely discussed within the volunteer literature (Aves 1969; Humble 1982; H. Jackson 1985) was underlined by the fact that another 17 per cent initially heard of the work from friends or relatives. In line with national findings, rather fewer mentioned volunteer bureaux or the media.

All the volunteers we interviewed were accredited to the probation service. In pure form this entailed submitting an application form and being interviewed by a probation officer, either at the probation offices or the applicant's home. Two satisfactory references were also required. In some cases the procedure was relaxed, often because the person was well known; many worked as unaccredited volunteers for a few months before finalizing their attachment through the accreditation system. Indeed, in some areas this was policy, giving prospective volunteers a chance to test their suitability.

Although there are no records available for failed applications, officers expressed concern at those who were either 'too authoritarian' or 'too easily taken advantage of'. Certainly some – in particular if they had received a bad reference, or in one case because of a previous conviction for shoplifting – were identified as warranting extra guidance or supervision. Most who applied though were accepted.

What then are the characteristics of these successful applicants? The records revealed that 56 per cent of volunteers were female, slightly lower than in Hereford and Worcester (Murgatroyd 1987) and Hull (Davidson et al. 1985). While this parallels findings for volunteers in general (Aves 1969; Humble 1982), especially when compared with the gender balance among probation officers (Walton 1975), we should reiterate Barr's (1971) concern that the contribution of a large minority of male volunteers should not be forgotten when the results are summarized.

Findings on marital and employment status also tended to support earlier conclusions on other samples of volunteers. Thus a large majority (69 per cent) were married, 76 per cent had children and half of these had school-age children. In the context of findings on gender and marital status it was not surprising to find that 20 per cent were housewives, which is in line with other studies (Davidson et al. 1985; Murgatroyd 1987). In contrast, though, rather more (50 per cent) were currently employed; 13 per cent were unemployed (less than Hull but more than Hereford and Worcester) and 7 per cent were students, broadly similar to Murgatroyd's (1987) finding but well below the 25 per cent found in Hull (Davidson et al. 1985).

The number of unemployed volunteers is very much in line with the regional picture. However, in terms of occupational status, probation volunteers were scarcely typical residents of the South-west and reflected a middle-class bias similar to that found for volunteers nationally (Humble 1982). Thus, data from probation records allowed us to categorize 57 per cent of volunteers as from social classes I and II, with 16 per cent III non-manual, 16 per cent III manual and only 11 per cent from classes IV and V. A similar picture emerged from the interview data, which also revealed distinctive patterns on educational careers, another indicator of status. Thus over two-thirds had pursued their education beyond the school-leaving age and 14 per cent had higher educational qualifications.

Data on age are also similar to those found for volunteers in general and by

Murgatroyd (1987) for probation, in contrast to the much younger group of volunteers in Hull, reflected in the number of students (Davidson *et al.* 1985). Thus only 14 per cent were aged 30 years or less, with half the interview sample aged 31–50 and 17 per cent aged 61 or more. Overall then, the results confirm those of previous writers here and abroad in indicating a middle-aged, middle-class, married, female bias.

So far then we have noted who the volunteers are and how they were accepted. At present we have said little about why someone should want to join the service as a volunteer, and yet this is of interest for at least two interrelated reasons. The first is that, as Barr (1971) has noted, probation clients are frequently considered 'undeserving' and certainly less deserving than other groups like the handicapped. So why do people want to help the undeserving? The second, and a point we shall return to in Chapter 6, concerns possible differences in the motivations of those who want to help offenders rather than, say, victims (like victim-support volunteers).

During the interviews we asked all our samples two questions: first, what had attracted them to voluntary work generally?; and second, why had they chosen that particular agency? The replies were coded into six categores which we have defined as 'other-directed', 'self-directed', 'career', 'organizational' or 'agency-directed', 'religious-based' and 'drift'.[8] We then went on to ask them about their reasons for continuing as probation volunteers. First, though, let us consider the reasons respondents gave for undertaking voluntary work.

The largest category, accounting for 26 per cent of replies, covered self-directed reasons; that is, where voluntary work was cited as of benefit to the volunteer. Three variations on this theme emerged. Some had wished for more interesting and demanding activities, some had felt it would help them to get to know other people, and others had experienced a need to get involved in something – or indeed *anything*. For example:

> I was staying in someone else's house and wanted an interest to take me away. (PV 08)

> My children had left home and I had time. I was not attracted to all female and all domestic activity. (PV 12)

> Before I came down here I was a Samaritan, but when I arrived I knew nothing about the area so I wanted to become involved. (PV 47)

A rather more specific type of self-directed reason is associated with career, where voluntary work is seen as a step on the ladder towards paid employment. In our sample, 22 per cent were so defined, in that they viewed their involvement in voluntary work as a prerequisite for pursuing a career in the welfare field, or in one instance the police service. A further 19 per cent cited other-directed reasons. For example:

> I like people and I like to try and help people. (PV 40)

Because you look forward and see so many in need who are incapable of helping themselves.   (PV 52)

This philanthropic motive is well documented in the literature. Less evident, in contrast, is an awareness that many may *drift* into voluntary work and indeed make no real conscious *decision* to volunteer. Among probation volunteers, some 19 per cent gave answers which implied that there had been no predetermined decision; they became volunteers when the opportunity arose at a point when they had time on their hands, for example:

My wife and I were at an evening class and a Probation Officer gave us a talk and it seemed worth doing.   (PV 37)

As already noted, a number gave reasons which were associated with career ambitions in probation or other welfare fields. In addition to these, 10 per cent gave answers which were organizational or agency directed. That is, they did not become involved in *voluntary* work so much as in *probation* work. For example:

When released from custody I came to probation and found they had an interest group which was my interest, and so I kept coming and they accredited me for expenses.   (PV 06)

Finally, two respondents (3 per cent) gave replies centred around their religious convictions. However, whilst this is only a small minority, clearly religion played an indirect part in the decisions made by many respondents. Thus over a quarter attended a place of worship at least fortnightly, over half said they held religious convictions, and 21 per cent said in reply to a direct question that their voluntary work was linked to their religious convictions. Religious factors do not appear to feature prominently as primary motivators, but they nevertheless may be considered an important contributory factor.

We subsequently asked why volunteers became involved in work with the probation service. In reply, 37 per cent cited organizational or agency-led reasons, 20 per cent career motives and 27 per cent indicated drift. At one extreme then are those who make conscious decisions to do probation work, at the other over a quarter saw probation work as just a form of voluntary activity in which they just happened to have become engaged. The following quotes, two from each, illustrate the distinction:

I was interested in why people commit crime, having been in the Police . . . I was keen to know the other side.   (PV 08)

I was interested in probation because I was interested in a playgroup they ran and it all stemmed from that.   (PV 46)

While a youth leader I had people on community service and that led to working with probation.   (PV 10)

The Intermediate Group led me on to probation, it was a snowball effect.   (PV 48)

The distinction is confirmed by a further question, where we asked respondents directly whether they were most interested in voluntary work in general or probation specifically; 43 per cent acknowledged a general interest, 52 per cent a specific commitment to probation.

The reasons why people originally became involved as volunteers may, however, be distinctly different from the reasons why they remain involved. Among probation volunteers, for example, only 9 per cent cited self-directed reasons for continuing. Rather more gave other-directed reasons, not all of which conformed to the stereotype of the caring welfare worker. For example:

> Because I want to. I am well organized and well able to help people. Most seem to have had a poor start in life and I feel I can put them on the right track. (PV 20)

> Two reasons. One, when I was in the Services I was a disciplinarian, and I think that youngsters need discipline. Two, I just like to see youngsters who have had a 'right do' with parents put in the right place. You must say there is more to life than getting drunk. (PV 34)

The largest number, accounting for 38 per cent, however, gave answers which indicated that they enjoyed what they were doing. For example:

> I enjoyed it, felt I was doing something worthwhile, which I hadn't previously. (PV 03)

> I think I am quite good at it, I enjoy it, and most of those I meet I enjoy meeting and would have met them no other way. Also I find it interesting. (PV 43)

Commitment, however, is sometimes strained by the working environment of the volunteer. As already noted, probation volunteers were especially critical of their under-use, and our national review identified scepticism among some officers. It is thus appropriate here to focus on the two sides of the professional–volunteer relationship, starting first with probation officers' views about volunteers.

PROBATION OFFICERS' PERCEPTIONS OF VOLUNTEERS

Taken together, the findings reported so far present a degree of ambiguity. On the one hand, probation services appear to recognize the value of volunteers. On the other hand, one of their values, representation of the community, is weakened where volunteers are distinctly unrepresentative of the community. Moreover, services reported a degree of hostility towards volunteers expressed by officers, and this parallels widespread findings that probation volunteers are under-used. In this context, the views of individual officers take on a particular significance.

Turning to our respondents, 59 per cent were male, slightly lower than in the two services as a whole (64 per cent). A majority (72 per cent) were married. Only 14 per cent were aged 30 or less, with 54 per cent aged 31–50. Thus, while officers were more commonly male and volunteers females, and very old officers were rare – and given that they were, by virtue of their occupation, middle class – on this basic level probation officrs and volunteers were not that dissimilar. Over three-quarters were main-grade officers, and approximately half had at least eleven years' practical experience in probation. All but one said they sometimes worked with probation volunteers[9] and 48 per cent said they spent some off-duty time socializing with them. Not surprisingly, they described a wide variety of tasks which volunteers undertook. For example:

The tasks undertaken within the group of ten are: wives' group, one-to-one befriendship, transport, court work, literacy tuition, handicraft groups, sail-training representative, art group in day centre, supervised access in civil cases. (PR 013)

Keyworkers with inmates, mediating the real world to prisoners, keeping them human by social contact. (PR 029)

Involved in running or helping to run various schemes for youngsters mostly in the area of craft work and various hobbies. (PR 050)

Support to lonely or isolated clients. (PR 053)

In this context, probation officers saw the aims of using volunteers as twofold. Volunteers provided a back-up service; in addition, they contributed their own distinctive blend of help and support:

To enlist client support from willing and able members of the community on a basis different from that of professional involvement. (PR 001)

To widen help available to clients. To involve the community. To tap resources otherwise unavailable. (PR 008)

They have time to fulfil the role of befriends in a less formal way. (PR 053)

1 Represent the community – not paid professional.
2 Offer time.
3 Personal talents.
4 Offer something significantly different and sometimes more appropriate than professional input. (PR 269)

Probation officers were then asked for their own personal attitude towards volunteers and, later in the questionnaire, the views of probation officers in general. Not surprisingly, replies to this second question were less positive. However, the overall picture was a favourable one. Thus, 49 per cent of respondents said they were themselves 'very favourably' disposed towards volunteers and 41 per cent said they were 'favourably' disposed. Their views are illustrated in Table 3.3 and by the following replies to an open-ended follow-up question:

> They can give time when needed which often I cannot. They are frequently more accepted by clients (coded very favourable).   (PR 267)

> No one person can be all things to all people. Volunteers add a variety of dimensions to our clients' lives (coded very favourable).   (PR 270)

> A probation officer is an increasingly scarce resource, but even if he wasn't he cannot be all things to all men, and should 'manage' whatever community resources he can bring to bear on the needs of offenders, aimed at reducing the caused factors of crime (coded favourable).   (PR 058)

> I enjoy the freshness and enthusiasm which they bring (coded favourable).   (PR 050)

Answers to the second question, on general attitudes of probation officers were less positive, although 60 per cent said that officers in general were favourably disposed and only 3 per cent said they were usually negative in their outlook. In general, respondents were critical of some of their colleagues, aware that some volunteers were better than others, and alive to the problems of volunteers identified in our national survey. These are well illustrated in the following quotes:

> Because they see them as a threat and as additional work.   (PR 005)

> Some officers have had bad experiences with unsuitable VAs who may be very demanding of POs' time themselves.   (PR 024)

> POs usually feel 'precious' about their caseloads and *can* see VAs as a threat.   (PR 035)

TABLE 3.3 Probation officers' perceptions of their relationships with probation volunteers

	Very favourable	Favourable	In-different	Don't know	Un-favourable	Very un-favourable
	%	%	%	%	%	%
Personal attitudes towards probation volunteers	49	41	10	0	0	0
General attitudes of probation officers towards volunteers	0	60	35	2	3	0
Volunteers' attitudes towards probation officers	11	72	11	3	3	0

1 There is the question of training and supervising. Some turn up (in past days) at the office at any hour, and expect a listening ear, irrespective of work pressures.

2 There is a strong feeling that if there were no vols, then our staff would be increased. The employers favour 'cheap labour'.   (PR 054)

Overall there thus appears to be some ambiguity in the attitudes of probation officers. On a general level, they are favourably disposed towards volunteers; however, they also recognize many of the problems which are associated with increased reliance on volunteers. Moreover, and this is also illustrated in Table 3.3, they generally felt that volunteers held positive views about them. This is reflected in the experiences of voluntary workers themselves.

VOLUNTEERS' PERCEPTIONS OF PROBATION OFFICERS

The ways in which volunteers were organized varied across the two services. However, notwithstanding the formal structure, it was most common for a particular probation officer to have considerable discretion over whether or not to work with volunteers, and where he or she did so, to depend on the one or two volunteers recognized as reliable. Indeed, nearly half our sample of volunteers worked with only one probation officer. Thus, even where in theory a group of volunteers were attached to a whole team, in practice volunteers tended to be associated with one probation officer who was considered a likely source of cases.

In order to assess this volunteer–professional relationship, volunteers were asked a similar series of questions to those for probation officers, namely: the attitude of probation officers to themselves personally and volunteers in general, and their own views of probation officers with whom they worked and officers in general.

Overall, as is shown clearly in Table 3.4, volunteers felt that relationships were good, although, as with officers, they were more positive about their own relationships than those of all probation volunteers.

Quite clearly volunteers believed that probation officers displayed positive attitudes towards them personally. As two explained:

I think we work very well together. We get on well.   (PV 14)

They treat me like another probation officer but without the pay.

(PV 21)

Others identified reasons in their own qualities! For example:

I seem to be one of the ones with a client straight away. Some were being used for transport and were without a client.   (PV 01)

TABLE 3.4 Probation volunteers' perceptions of their relationships with probation officers

	Very favour- able	Favour- able	In- different	Don't know	Un- favour- able	Very un- favour- able
	%	%	%	%	%	%
Probation officers' attitudes towards them	52	38	4	7	0	0
Probation officers' attitudes towards volunteers in general	22	53	11	15	0	0
Own views of officers with whom they worked	54	35	2	7	2	0
Views volunteers in general held about officers	11	54	5	26	4	0

I am pleasant, I am willing, I am caring. I believe I am good as a volunteer. I ask questions when I don't know, I report back, and I am not afraid to make myself heard if necessary. That all adds up to be positive. Also I have been reliable, I have turned up. Well, you did ask!   (PV 17)

Those who answered indifferently or were not sure of an answer reasoned that variations in attitudes between probation officers made generalizations difficult. As two noted:

Extremely mixed. The one I work with most was extremely helpful. Others I thought were unhelpful. There was a great feeling of threat among probation officers, but they (volunteers) are becoming more common now.   (PV 12)

The last probation officer resented us and was always undermining what we were doing, but the new one is marvellous – nothing is too much trouble (and) asks our advice.   (PV 43)

This aspect was further developed in the answers volunteers gave to the question on officers' attitudes to volunteers in general. Some took this a stage further and noted that the haphazard way in which they were organized as a group was indicative of a certain amount of antipathy. For example, two who described that attitude as indifferent noted:

Reading between the lines I get the impression there is not a lot of consideration.   (PV 56)

If you are going to use Voluntary Associates that needs a bit of your time. It is not highly organized and that makes things difficult.   (PV 57)

Criticisms of levels of training, under-use, poor organization and the indifference of some probation officers might be anticipated to be reflected in direct criticism of officers. However, on the contrary respondents viewed those they knew as a meritorious group and paid tribute to their commitment:

They are all brilliant. Never had any trouble with any of them.   (PV 06)

I think they are fantastic, very professional. No criticism whatsoever.

(PV 14)

I respect them. I like the way they do their job.   (PV 51)

Again, here, there were caveats, with volunteers stressing the degree of variation from officer to officer. But most thought that other volunteers too felt positively about probation officers. For example:

They respect the professionals for what they do and appreciate they have a difficult job.   (PV 32)

Most appreciate the difficult job they have, and they are working for the good of the client.   (PV 41)

Nevertheless among these and less positive respondents there were those who expressed a mixture of approval and discontent over lack of work. Typical replies included:

Frustrated at the lack of things to do. You are continually wondering why you are doing this. It must be favourable otherwise they would not do it.

(PV 32)

They all complained about not being used enough, this is the only thing. It also depends on the area.   (PV 49)

What is also of significance here, though, is that over a quarter felt unable to say how other volunteers felt. The lack of a training programme and high rates of inactivity limited the extent to which volunteers met other volunteers to reflect on how typical their own experiences were. Overall, 36 per cent said they had no friends who were probation officers and 45 per cent that they had no friends among probation volunteers; only just over a quarter said they socialized with either officers *or* volunteers (and some of these sometimes interpreted the question to include one-off Christmas or office parties).

We are able to comment further on some of the intricacies of the volunteer–professional relationship through our observational work. Without doubt there were considerable variations in attitudes amongst officers, while volunteers, although lamenting their under-use, still displayed an extremely positive attitude towards probation officers. Variations amongst officers is perhaps not surprising in the light of previous research. Nevertheless, there were certainly a number of different reasons behind this.

The issue of lack of work, and by implication the lack of enthusiasm of some officers, was a frequent topic of discussion at volunteer meetings. Often the officers attending these meetings were required to proffer explanations, and a variety of points were mentioned. Autonomy is a case in point. Many admitted that they had, through their training, been encouraged to see clients as *their* responsibility. Consequently the idea of sharing with a volunteer was alien. For example, on one occasion an officer was talking about the role of volunteers in working with clients on a long-term basis, and contended: 'The kind of task a probation officer finds difficult to allocate, probation officers get possessive. We sometimes feel we are the experts with all the knowledge and find it difficult to pass on responsibility.'

On another occasion, in the context of a direct question from a volunteer on the attitude of officers, the professional was quite blatant about the issue of autonomy: 'Some probation officers don't use volunteers because they are jealous of their own responsibilities. I tend to give them work which I have not the time or skills for.'

Not surprisingly therefore, some officers, when using volunteers, were keen to identify strict guidelines as to the role of the volunteer, making it clear there should be no secrets. In consequence, a frequent topic of discussion at meetings concerned the extent to which volunteers should pass on information to a probation officer, or anyone else for that matter. Again opinions varied widely on the principle, on both the side of the volunteer and the professional. While there is not space here to develop this further, we would suggest more generally that a lack of clarity about what a volunteer would or should do in these types of situations hindered the integration of volunteers into the probation service.

Clarifying the role of volunteers may well be a stepping stone to increasing their acceptability to officers. Indeed, it would be a mistake to believe that all antipathy, where it existed, was so ingrained as to be almost beyond remedy. Often very small administrative changes could overcome what might otherwise be interpreted as a lack of probation-officer interest. This too was often raised at volunteer meetings and, as one probation officer suggested in discussion with volunteers, the problem may well be as much administrative as structural: 'I have to admit we are not really volunteer conscious. We have got your names and addresses but we haven't really seen them as a source of contact for cases.'

On this occasion, as on so many others at meetings throughout the research area, a decision was taken to remedy the situation. This often involved circulating names, addresses and interests of volunteers to all probation staff. Rarely, though, did it show any marked effect. On the one hand it is possible to interpret this as an inherent dislike of volunteers by professionals. On the other hand it may suggest that the administration and organization process was flawed. We favour the latter view, and we shall readdress the issue in Chapter 7.

Here it is perhaps timely to consider briefly those who resigned from their voluntary work with the probation service during the research period. Although details are available for only 19 respondents, a fairly clear picture emerges. Those who left tended to be rather younger than volunteers in general, and 79 per cent had been volunteers with the service for no more than three years. Most had found the experience 'very enjoyable' (63 per cent) or enjoyable (32 per cent), and 42 per cent thought they would probably rejoin as volunteers in the future. Contact with other volunteers and probation officers were no less than for our sample of current volunteers. Only one thought probation volunteers were unnecessary. However, three felt their views of the service had changed for the worse during their time as volunteers. Thus, while most left for reasons associated with changing circumstances, a few were provoked by what they saw as unsympathetic staff or inadequate organizations. For example:

> I have commitments that I have decided were more important than the role I was asked to fulfil. . . . My decision may have been different if the day centre I was working in had been organized, funded and backed in a more efficient way. The officer in charge did not help or encourage VAs to get involved by the way VAs were treated. The communication between staff, VAs and clients was totally non-existent, and the VAs constantly found meetings that were arranged, and they had given their time up to attend, cancelled without them being informed, so hence morale was always low.   (PVL 017)

This view is certainly not typical of former probation volunteers, but it none the less illustrates an extreme which may *occur* if volunteers do not consider themselves to be valued. Overall we feel that the probation services demonstrated an inefficient use of volunteers as resources and an ironically insensitive response to volunteers as people.

SUMMARY

In moving from the international literature through the national picture to our own locally based research, it is evident that some issues receive more attention in one context than in others. In particular, we have focused rather more on volunteers' motives for joining the probation service than have others, with the possible exception of Gandy's (1977) Canadian research and there is more emphasis in the North American literature on assessing effectiveness. Nevertheless, we find some themes expressed in similar terms (and indeed with similar conclusions) across a variety of environments: the type of work considered suitable for volunteers, the social characteristics of volunteers, the ways in which they are organized and problems concerning professional–volunteer relationships emerge time and time again as central issues.

It is clear that some probation volunteers are actively involved in a variety of projects involving a diverse range of probation clients. In some cases there is close liaison with a probation officer, and in some areas a training programme is supplemented by useful volunteer meetings. It is important to stress that this does occur. At the same time, much of our evidence paints a somewhat different and far less rosy picture of the place of volunteers in probation.

The alternative picture has in the foreground willing helpers being engaged by the service and then provided with little, or irregular, work. In the background there may be a training programme: if so it will be disorganized, and this is also true of volunteer meetings where, often, only the co-ordinating officer will attend. Laments at under-use will be met with the promise of change, but this is commonly an illusion. Even when there is a referral of a client, there is no guarantee that supervision will be freely available. Despite the obvious indifference of some officers, though, volunteers remain positive about the probation service and especially about the probation officers with whom they worked.

These two pictures co-exist. That all or more volunteers are not actively involved in the service, and that so many are treated insensitively is, we would argue, as much to do with organization as with any ingrained hostility. Before we consider this in detail, we turn to review the experiences of volunteers in a very different context, policing, and assess how far similar issues arise in this contrasting environment.

4

THE SPECIAL
CONSTABULARY

HISTORICAL INTRODUCTION

We have already discussed in Chapter 1 the processes whereby the community policing systems of Anglo-Saxon England were gradually transformed, by means of a mixture of public, private and informal structures, into the statutory conglomerate of local policing systems which distinguished England and Wales from much of Europe. However, as we have detailed elsewhere (Gill and Mawby 1990), the special constabulary originated, not as a community or voluntary system of policing, but as a paid police reserve.

The idea of special constables can be traced back to an act of 1662[1] whereby members of the public could be sworn in as paid constables for a specified term to meet a local emergency. Nevertheless the modern special constabulary can more appropriately be traced back to the Special Constables Act of 1831. While we have dealt with an historical study of the specials elsewhere (Gill and Mawby 1990), it is worth drawing attention here to the range of events that have justified their use in the last century and a half or so.

In the early years the use of specials was very much allied to local or national emergencies: they have not always been an adjunct to day-to-day policing. Leon (1987) has noted that specials were used in the early 1830s in response to a spate of arson attacks in the South-east. They were also regularly deployed throughout London:

> The enlistment of special constables varied in proportion to the gravity of the emergency. An incipient unrest, or a disturbance confined to a relatively narrow locality, usually had the effect of prompting the magistrates of the district to call out on their own initiatives ten, fifteen, or twenty of the most respectable inhabitants to strengthen the hands of the civil power. But when

public order was endangered over a wide area of the Metropolis the initiative passed from the magistrates to the Home Office. Then the enlistment of special constables assumed the character of an organized mobilization.

(Radzinowicz 1956b: 218)

However, the establishment of regular forces had a more direct effect on day-to-day policing patterns than on emergencies and there was still a need for auxiliary forces to meet special circumstances. Special constables were thus, for example, deployed in numbers at the Chartist demonstration at Kennington Common in 1848, the Reform League's public meeting in Hyde Park in 1867 and to help the regular police during the Fenian disorders of 1867–8 (P. T. Smith 1985). Special constables also featured significantly during the police strikes of 1918 and 1919 and the General Strike of 1926. They were also crucial to order maintenance during the 1914–18 and 1939–45 world wars (Critchley 1978; Seth 1961). The First World War also signalled the beginning of a shift towards the use of specials as a permanent police reserve and saw for the first time the involvement of women in policework, principally in two separate agencies, the Women Police Volunteers and Voluntary Women's Patrols (Critchley 1978; Jones 1986; Owings 1969).

The special constabulary in Britain today varies considerably from these early origins; specials are, for example, normally unpaid[2] and women are integrated into the service (Gill and Mawby 1990). Perhaps most significantly though, there has been a shift in balance from a situation where a large number of volunteers were registered as a police reserve to be deployed only on an episodic basis, to the current position where a much smaller group of volunteers provide a regular contribution as a supplement to the police service. The balance between a police reserve and the routine use of volunteers is important in the context of the international picture.

THE INTERNATIONAL SCENE

In fact, some countries, in other respects strongly influenced by the British criminal justice system, appear to have seen little use for a volunteer force either as a reserve or on a regular basis. In Canada, for example, although the Toronto and Vancouver police deploy police reserves, in many areas there appears to be minimal use, and even less discussion over any sort of auxiliary police. In the light of such ambivalence, police suspicion of any suggestion to develop substantial volunteer units seems to have been decisive (Willett and Chitty 1982). Closer to home, and at the other extreme, Jersey's dependence on volunteer police, growing from similar roots to that in mainland Britain, has produced a very different specimen (Gill and Mawby 1990).

In general, those societies which have a history of encouraging community involvement in law enforcement on an informal level have tended to be most willing to design police volunteer programmes. In Japan, for example, crime-prevention associations organize street patrols and the police are also heavily involved in screening volunteers working with a variety of criminal justice agencies as youth assistants, probation aides, prison visitors and traffic assistants (Ames 1979; Bayley 1976). In China, the neighbourhood-based crime-prevention work of the Security Defence Small Groups is supplemented by police volunteer units, known as Volunteer People's Militia in the countryside and People's Patrols in the cities. The latter, which originally concentrated on traffic-related issues, subsequently became involved in other general public-order policing and child-neglect cases (Cohen 1968). Similarly in Cuba there are both street-level citizen units, the Committees for the Defence of the Revolution (CDRs) and police auxiliaries who are attached to the police and augment police strength. Membership is more restricted than for CDRs and auxiliaries carry weapons and have the same arrest powers as the police (Berman 1969; Salas 1979).

Organized citizen involvement in crime control may thus be located within semi-autonomous neighbourhood groups like the CDR, the Security Defence Small Groups, or – in the United States and Britain – neighbourhood watch, or alternatively subsumed within the police organization itself, as with police volunteer forces. However, while the United States has been a major growth area for neighbourhood watch (Bennett 1987; Figgie Report 1983), use of police volunteers is less evident and of more recent origin than in England and Wales. Indeed, the need for a reserve force in emergencies has commonly been met either through the involvement of other permanent units of social control or through a paid part-time reserve force.

Greenberg (1978) traces the origins of police volunteers in the USA back to the civil-defence units of the First World War, whilst Gourley and Bristow (1970) also note the impetus provided by the policing requirements of the prohibition period, and subsequently the Second World War and the Korean conflict. Since then, certainly, volunteers have been utilized by a range of police departments across the United States and have undertaken a variety of duties. In Geauga County, Ohio, for example, the auxiliary unit is split into six squads covering road patrol, detection, communication, records, maintenance and situational (including jail) duties (Todd and Smith 1983). The extent of training varies considerably, in relation to the types of duties expected of volunteers and whether they are accredited with arms (Berg and Doerner 1987; Sherwood 1980). At the extreme, the training period in Dade County covers 340 hours over a nine-month period, after which volunteers are eligible for entry into the full-time force (Bohart 1977).

Frequently the characteristics of volunteers are similar to those of regular officers. Thus Berg and Doerner (1987), Sundeen and Siegel (1986) and Bohart (1977) describe typical volunteers as white males in their 30s in full-time employment, with relatively good educational backgrounds. However, Greenberg (1978) stresses that auxiliaries in New York tended to include rather more blacks, Puerto Ricans, Jews and Chinese than did the regular police. While, as we shall note below, this concern with representatives, particularly in terms of ethnic balance, is not unfamiliar in England and Wales, in at least one respect experiences from the United States are somewhat different. That is, while in countries such as Cuba, Japan and (latterly) Britain police-volunteer use is identified as a facet of community involvement in the law-enforcement process, with advantageous implications, in the United States there appears in addition to be a more significant and more explicit focus on cost-saving advantages (Deitch and Thompson 1985; Todd and Smith 1983). Discussions of police volunteers and neighbourhood watch, with few exceptions (Sundeen and Siegel 1986) thus appear on quite separate agendas.

THE NATIONAL PICTURE

In 1987 there were over 16,000 special constables in England and Wales, approximately 32.4 per 100,000 population or 13.1 per 100 police officers (Home Office 1988: 86). A direct comparison with probation is instructive on two counts. First, clearly the number of volunteers working with the police far exceeds that for probation. Second, and in marked contrast, the number of volunteers compared with paid employees is considerably smaller; that is, the numerical significance of volunteers within the organization is less.

As will by now be evident, there is at least one further difference. Whereas the use of volunteers within probation has been increasing, the police has experienced a post-war decline. Since 1961, as dramatic increases in recorded crime have been matched by moderate increases in police personnel, the number of specials declined steadily until the early 1980s. In 1961, for example, there were 62.8 specials for every 100 regular officers – over four times the present position (Central Statistical Office 1988: 196).

Clearly not all of this decline is to be viewed negatively. After the war many specials became inactive or were called on infrequently. Some remained on the books for the limited status and perks. However, they subsequently came to be defined as 'dead wood' and the falling numbers partially reflect the outcome of a 'weeding out' process. Nevertheless, it was also recognized that the police were losing potential volunteers to other organizations. As the Police Advisory Board (1981: 2–3) accepted: 'Many people interested in service to the community tend to be drawn to work with the under-privileged or handicapped rather than to the more controversial area of law and order.'

Moreover, at a time when recruitment is afforded new priority, area variations attain particular significance. As with probation, while variations in numbers of paid employees result from negotiations between local management and the Home Office, the number of volunteers is dependent upon both local management policies and the availability of suitable applicants. It is possible to consider the outcome of these two influences by analysing data for each police authority, available from the *Report of Her Majesty's Chief Inspector of Constabulary 1987* (Home Office 1988) incorporating recorded crime data from

Criminal Statistics for England and Wales (Home Office 1986). We are consequently able to compare the distribution of special constables for the 43 police authorities in England and Wales (the Metropolitan and City forces in London are combined for this purpose).

Just as for probation, area variations are considerable. For example, the lowest rates per 100,000 population were to be found in South Wales (16.5), Greater Manchester (17.9), South Yorkshire (21.0) and London (21.2) and the highest in Warwickshire (73.6), Lincolnshire (63.7) and Devon and Cornwall (56.7). Using the number of specials per 100 regular officers as a measure, a similar picture emerges, with the lowest rates in London (5.5), Greater Manchester (6.5) and South Wales (6.7) and the highest rates in Warwickshire (35.4), Lincolnshire (30.0) and Devon and Cornwall (28.8).

What then of any consistency? Statistical analysis reveals two quite distinct patterns for the number of regular officers and special constables. Regular establishment levels are higher in more densely populated police authorities with higher recorded crime rates – reflecting the formula on appropriate strengths developed by the Home Office. In contrast, the number of specials per 100,000 population is greater in police authorities with low density and low recorded crime rates.

Clearly ecological analysis is fraught with difficulties. Nevertheless, it seems that whereas statutory services may be varied and adjusted to meet variations in area need, dependence upon volunteers brings with it the danger that volunteers will not be available where needs are greatest. That is, in densely populated areas where crime rates (or at least recorded rates) are highest, volunteer potential may be low. In contrast, in more rural areas with lower crime rates volunteers may be relatively plentiful. The situation is not dissimilar from that described by Mather (1959) in the Chartist period.

In fact, whilst there is little or no published academic research in Britain on the contemporary state of the special constabulary, *official debate* has centred on the twin questions of declining numbers and imbalance. For example, in the Metropolitan Police, Hope and Lloyd's (1984) research was geared towards concern that low recruitment figures were cancelled out by wastage and that the representation of specials in certain areas of London and among racial-minority groups was particularly low. More recently, government enthusiasm for revitalizing the special constabulary (Hogg 1988; Home Office 1987) has also centred on recruitment but has also incorporated a review of the most appropriate ways of deployment. This aspect is also reflected in our own contacts with a number of forces.

What then do we know about the special constabulary? The answer is very little in terms of details of the characteristics of police volunteers. Recorded data cover only gender. In this respect, a majority (67 per cent) of specials in 1987 were male, but this was less than for the regular police (90 per cent) (Home Office 1988: 86).

Rather more is known of the work carried out by specials in Britain today.

This falls under three main headings. First is the traditional function of acting as a reserve force for times of emergency. Training and duties are therefore geared towards the eventuality that they might have to assume the police function. Second, and partly related to this, is work as a police reserve when special, perhaps seasonal, events require a larger police presence than is practical from the regular force. Third, it is increasingly acknowledged that specials have a role to play as an adjunct to the police in their local communities, particularly in relation to crime-prevention initiatives such as neighbourhood watch.

The role of specials in West Yorkshire neighbourhood-watch schemes has received considerable coverage (Home Office 1987: 9–10; Newton 1987). This involves specials working locally under the guidance of community police officers, patrolling their own area 'and to act as a focal point in each neighbourhood for self help and crime prevention initiatives' (Home Office 1987: 9–10). A number of other forces also use specials in this type of work and one area informed us that they were also represented on local crime-prevention panels.

This emphasis is of relatively recent origin and in some forces specials have been recruited specifically to work with neighbourhood-watch schemes. Indeed, syndicate discussion at the Home Office (1987: 23) Conference reflected:

(A) danger that the community role e.g. in Neighbourhood Watch could come to overshadow the very important and core emergency reserve function. It was suggested that the best approach was to consider the duties to be performed by the Constabulary as a whole rather than attempt to split the time of individual Specials into various types of duty.

This generic alternative is reflected in an experiment in Norfolk, where specials were given responsibility for the total policing of an area, resulting in 'benefits to the community and the Special Constabulary from such exercises' (Home Office 1987: 17). Subsequent syndicate discussions supported this idea:

Experience of driving, foot patrol, plain clothes duty, work in the custody suite, the mundane and routine administrative functions – the full range – would all help to ensure that Specials were effective when the resources of the regular force were stretched in an emergency.

(Home Office 1987: 23)

Forces vary in the extent to which they allow specials access to specialist departments. Equally, regulation of the number of hours work done by volunteers varies considerably. For example, one constabulary noted that, 'each special is expected to perform at least 4 hours duty per *month* but should not exceed 4 hours per week'; while another specified 'under normal circumstances a maximum of 12 hours duty should not be exceeeded in any one week'; this latter service did require 'a minimum of 25 hours *operational* duty per year in addition to formal training sessions'.[3]

This is probably lower than in most other forces, but the overall tendency is to request a *regular* rather than a minimum contribution. Another relevant issue is specials' experience and ability, often related to training. The Police Advisory Board (1981) set out a series of guidelines on the importance of training which appear to be followed by most forces, although there are variations – for example, in the importance placed on residential courses, or the extent to which training is focused on new recruits or experienced supervisory specials. Very often training is linked to special operations like the 'take-over days' described above.

Whether specials are recruited as a general police reserve or as a part of a project like neighbourhood watch also has implications for recruitment policies, as the Metropolitan Police found (Hope and Lloyd 1984). In fact, there a number of initiatives were used, including saturation exposure of targeted areas, with specials involved in a formalized local campaign. This has been supplemented by media coverage and the production of a recruitment video. A medley of alternative recruitment strategies is displayed by Greater Manchester. There policies have included advertisements in the local press, divisional and HQ open evenings, civilian staff circulars, display stands, and the appointment of a special in each division as a recruitment officer (Home Office 1987).

This recent emphasis on recruitment reflects the new-found importance being given to the special constabulary. In official terms, its viability combines at least three elements – the need to have a trained reserve ready in times of emergency; the extent to which volunteers can be used as an alternative to increased state spending; finally a growing awareness of the importance of the public as part of the policing process. Additionally, as the Home Office (1987) conference realized, the special constabulary is increasingly providing a route for individuals entering the regular force, particularly advantageous where – following Scarman (1981) and indicative of some literature from the United States – it might attract a wider cross-section of the community.

There is, within official documentation, little to balance this with regard to the disadvantages of dependence upon specials. Interestingly it is revealed more in the context of reassurance given that potential difficulties will not be allowed to arise. In particular, government ministers have stressed the need for specials to be well trained and display overall competence, and the need to ensure that they would not be used as a replacement for paid labour (Hogg 1988; Home Office 1987). Certainly these were the two major issues to emerge from our analysis of *Police Review* whose letters pages have, over the years bristled with correspondence from regular officers concerned at the general incompetence of specials and the threat which they might pose to overtime levels. However, these issues are rarely addressed directly in the available literature and are therefore given particular prominence in our own research reported below.

THE USE OF POLICE SPECIALS IN DEVON AND CORNWALL

The counties of Devon and Cornwall comprise one police authority with its headquarters in Exeter. It is perhaps best known for its popularization of the principles of community policing, promoted by its former chief constable John

Alderson (1979; see also Moore and Brown 1981). Certainly, in Alderson's work, there is explicit recognition of the link between community policing and a planned, constructive use of the special constabulary, and it is not surprising therefore to note that the force has one of the highest rates of specials in the country.

Equally, as with probation, there are marked variations within the force. The rate per 100,000 electorate is highest in Devon West and Torridge (167.9), followed by Truro (126.2). At the other extreme again are the three Plymouth constituencies – Drake (19.0), Devonport (20.4) and, to a lesser extent, the predominantly middle-class Sutton (35.9). However, in contrast to probation, Exeter has a relatively low rate of specials.

Despite this, a Pearson correlation analysis reveals a positive association between rates of probation volunteers and special constables. Moreover, specials are also more common in constituencies with higher social-class profiles. Again then, there is evidence that even within a force with a comparatively large number of specials, some areas – including the most urban – are somewhat less fertile sources of recruitment than others.

What then of the ways in which specials are organized and managed in the force? First, it must be stressed that, as with the regular force, specials are organized on a divisional basis, each being headed by a divisional commandant, with sub-divisional officers and section officers constituting the remainder of the specials' separate hierarchy. On the regulars' side, the divisional training sergeant is responsible for co-ordinating the work of the specials, and it is his or her responsibility to organize and run training programmes and deal with other day-to-day issues.

Divisions are where policies are applied, and at this and at station level there exist considerable variations in practices. In some small stations an annual rota was operated; in others specials might be assigned for, say, two regular terms of duty each month; in others specials would work only on specified weekends. At one extreme, the common practice in some stations was for specials to ring up when they wanted to go on duty.

Local practices thus influenced the extent to which specials could become involved. At one station, where specials were particularly well integrated, they explained to one of us how a nearby station never used volunteers because it was 'anti-special'. Overall, however, there was no lack of enthusiasm among specials. Only three of our sample were inactive at the time of interview and three-quarters committed more than two hours of their time weekly. Moreover, eight-hour shifts were not uncommon and one special to whom we spoke said that he had on one occasion undertaken 16 hours of consecutive policework![4]

Work patterns were to some extent influenced by the type of work carried out. This tended to fall into three categories. First, there were a series of administrative responsibilities – ordering uniforms, processing travelling expenses, liaising with regulars, etc. – which tended to fall on a small number of graded officers. More common were duties at special events – like carnivals, fetes or football matches – where specials were deployed on traffic duty or crowd control. Whilst practically all specials had at some point been involved in this work, the third category, routine patrolling, was the most common, and it is worth focusing on it in a little more detail here.

Our data confirm the views of the Police Advisory Board (1976) Working Party that patrols were most commonly carried out with regular officers rather than other specials. Indeed, about two-thirds of our sample said they normally patrolled with a regular officer. This took the form of doubling up and acting as observer in a panda car, or partnering an officer on foot patrol. However few were attached to the same officer regularly and, while Alderson's (1978) idea of specials' attaching themselves to their local community police officer was in evidence, it was rare.

This raises the question of whether specials would want or be prepared to work within their own community. During the interview a question was included on the extent to which specials were included in patrolling (either on foot or in a car) their own neighbourhood. In total, only 12 per cent had never done so, and the vast majority, 65 per cent, said they did 'sometimes' patrol their own neighbourhood. Very few were able to indicate any difficulties that had arisen, and even those who did considered them minor inconveniences (such as threats or rude comments) rather than serious problems. Moreover, all of 82 per cent who were known as a special in their neighbourhood considered this to be an advantage. In addition, of those who did not patrol their neighbourhood, only one was not prepared to do so. It thus appears from our findings that policing initiatives which call for greater local community participation could make better use of the special constabulary.

Whilst routine patrolling was the most common form of activity for specials, a fourth category, incorporating a range of specialist activities, although rarer, was important for other reasons. Occasionally specials would take on these other duties. Some managed to gain attachment to the Criminal Investigations Department (CID) but this was uncommon and was very much dependent on 'putting oneself about' and 'getting to know the right people'. A few had escorted prisoners to prison, but again this was rare. Nevertheless, tasks such as these, partly because they were out of the ordinary, partly because they were perceived as involving 'real police work', were extremely popular.

Generally speaking then specials could be categorized as assistants to regular officers, complementing their role and rarely involved in the 'hard' end of policing; indeed only 16 per cent had ever made an arrest themselves and over a quarter had never been involved in an arrest at all. Asked what they considered to be the role of the special constabulary, every respondent highlighted its value as a 'back up' or support to the regular force, with many seeing this as preparation for emergencies. Some typical comments were:

A reserve force to back up regulars in times of stress, and all the work must be training for times of stress and training for professionalism.   (SC04)

To assist all the regular force in any way they can, in every aspect of police study and to know police rules or regulations in case there was a time when the Specials had to take over.   (SC25)

To assist the regular force. To help new constables to get into the area. Also to help with the various village affairs where the regulars cannot cope, although I would never do the regulars out of overtime.   (SC07)

In discussing the work of police specials in Devon and Cornwall we have seen a commitment to assisting the regular force which extends to working in a variety of ways involving one's own community. However, this raises a number of questions. For example, how representative are specials of 'their' communities, and indeed, how well represented in the special constabulary are members of the mosaic of local communities found within a police authority? In this context, we shall move on to consider the type of people who became specials and their reasons for volunteering for policework.

POLICE SPECIALS

Much of the impetus behind the national debate on the future role of the special constabulary has been a concern with falling numbers and a corresponding emphasis on recruitment. This is well illustrated in the Action Plan initiated by the Commissioners of the Metropolitan Police in 1983–4 (Hope and Lloyd 1984). It is therefore perhaps surprising that the first Police Advisory Board (1976) Working Party considered it unnecessary to draw up guidelines for recruitment, preferring to emphasize the benefits of local initiatives. True, the Home Office do launch national recruitment campaigns and provide each police station with publicity material in order to advertise the work of the specials. But for the most part, as the Police Advisory Board for Scotland (1975) indicated, most specials are attracted either by regulars or other specials, emphasizing once again the prominence of the word-of-mouth recruitment method.

However, little is known about the selection process of those who volunteer their services. Certainly, there are guidelines within which they must work. The Police Advisory Board (1976) suggested minimum and maximum age limits, and there may, according to the wishes of the chief constable, be physical requirements in the form of height, eye-sight, etc. The Police Advisory Board (1981) underlined the importance of selecting the 'right people' by recommending that all applicants should undertake a recruitment test.

It would thus seem advantageous to review the recruitment strategies employed by the Devon and Cornwall police. Methods varied considerably throughout the force, being dependent not only on the willingness of training sergeants to commit time to this issue, but also on initiatives taken by specials themselves. In some areas, where the local police organized, or were involved in night schools or open days, specials were afforded the opportunity to be represented to outline the role of the police reserve. In one division the training sergeant and the divisional commandant developed an innovative idea of attending all the summer fairs and fetes, etc., in their area to advertise the special constabulary. With considerable organization they arranged for local specials to be photographed by 'scenes of crime' at distinguished and recognizable places within the division. It was hoped that, by this method, the public could identify the work of the specials with their own community and thereby it would serve the dual purpose of attracting attention to their work and encourage others to develop an interest in becoming a special. This initiative was backed up by the force commandant's appearing on local television advertising the special constabulary. Such appeals, however, were rare. For the most part the police relied on casual enquiries from the general public. Many specials stated during the course of the research that they initially heard and/or were encouraged to apply to the constabulary by another (former) special or regular. This then would suggest further support for the contention that word of mouth is the most common form of volunteer recruitment.

The selection process itself, although subject to area variations, shared common elements in terms of being rigorous and time consuming, rarely being completed within six months. A typical selection process was as follows. The completed application form was assessed by the training sergeant who would deal with any obvious problems pertaining to the applicant's suitability. If the applicant lacked the minimum educational qualifications he/she was invited to sit the Police Initial Recruitment (PIR) test.[5] Having passed their test, candidates were then visited at their home, sometimes by the community constables, sometimes by a sergeant (or even an inspector) and in some areas both of these. Frequently a graded special would accompany them, usually a sub-divisional officer. As one training sergeant remarked, the main purpose of the visit was to see what they looked like and whether their house was clean and tidy. Other assets being sought were 'character', 'confidence', 'motive', 'bearing', and 'enthusiasm'. References were always taken up: sometimes, and where it was possible, referees were interviewed by a constable. With all this information, a recommendation was made to the chief superintendent and subject to agreement, forwarded to headquarters for processing. The new special was then required to attend court for attestation and be fitted and supplied with a police uniform before being allowed to start work as a police officer.

The selection process is certainly an exhaustive one. Recently recruited specials who were interviewed informally throughout the research period often reflected with disillusionment on the length of the selection process, although, that aside, many stated that they were 'proud' to have been accepted. It was proof to them that not everyone could become a special and may have contributed to building up a sense of purpose about being involved in the police reserve. Similarly, the rigour with which the application process was applied and the fact that it should be so rigorous in the first instance are reflections of the emphasis the police place on recruiting and may therefore serve as a *rite of passage* to the occupational culture.

What then of the outcome in terms of the characteristics of accepted volunteers? The first point to note, which distinguishes specials from most volunteer groups, is that, according to the records, 79 per cent were male, even higher than the national figures. Three-quarters were married and over two-thirds had children, mostly of school age.

Data on employment status were equally striking. The records revealed that less than 1 per cent were classified as unemployed; however, half were classified as in social class III, with 28 per cent from classes I and II and 23 per cent from IV and V. Interview data revealed a similar pattern, confirming that in this respect specials were rather more typical of the local population than are most groups of volunteers. Equally, in details of education, 30 per cent had no qualification whatsoever.

Finally here, we can consider data on age. The Police Advisory Board (1976) had recommended a minimum age of 18.5 and a maximum of 55, which clearly limits the number of more elderly volunteers. Partly as a result of this, only 14 per cent of those we interviewed were aged 51 or more, with 35 per cent aged 41–50, and roughly a quarter in each of the categories 31–40 and 30 or less.

In all then, specials tended to be lower middle or skilled working class, middle aged, married and male. Whilst in some respects they do conform to the stereotype identified by Aves (1969), in others, notably gender and social class, they are somewhat distinctive, suggesting that the appeal of voluntary work with the police is qualitatively different from much other voluntary work.

As with probation volunteers, we first asked our sample of specials what had attracted them initially to voluntary work.

As many as 43 per cent gave answers we later categorized as self-directed reasons. For example:

Spare time on my hands and wanted to do something totally different.

(SC40)

I like to become involved in things. I think everyone should be involved in something. . . .   (SC38)

The next largest category contained those who were interested in the police as an organization. In other words, their decision to volunteer could not be isolated from their interest in the police. These accounted for 20 per cent of the sample. In each case these proportions were greater than for probation volunteers. However, the proportions citing other-directed reasons (18 per cent) and drift (18 per cent) were similar to those from probation. In contrast, no one claimed that work with the special constabulary was inspired *primarily* by religious beliefs, although 41 per cent did claim to be religious. In stark contrast to probation, only 4 per cent saw their voluntary work as a career route.

This is interesting because both locally and nationally – following Scarman (1981) – recent initiatives have been directed at using the special constabulary as a means of recruitment to the regulars, and it may be that a future picture will look very different. We did, in contrast, find a number of specials who had at some time in the past considered joining as regular officers but had not done so for some reason or other. For example:

I always fancied being in the police but had a height problem so I decided to go on a voluntary basis.   (SC34)

I was very friendly with the training sergeant. I always wanted to join the police but went into the navy and come out at the age of 27, married, and the police were not interested in me. So I joined the Specials at a later date when it was suggested.   (SC17)

For some then joining the specials was something of a consolation prize! The overall pattern, however, is one in which organizational or agency-led reasons were predominant. Thus, when asked directly whether they had been motivated to join the police specifically or had seen it as just one form of voluntary work, 77 per cent gave police specific answers. This finding is backed up by replies to our second question on motivations asking why respondents volunteered to work specifically with the police. A majority, 59 per cent, gave organizational or agency-directed replies. A further 28 per cent were considered to have drifted into work with the police. For example:

Originally I tried to join the fire service but the firm said no. I was quite friendly with PCs and they encouraged me to join.   (SC20)

If I had been near the sea I would have joined the lifeboats, if a fire station I would have joined them; I was near a police station.   (SC43)

In contrast to probation volunteers then, police specials were particularly attracted by the police organization, its image as an upholder of law and order, and the work.

Asked why they continued with their voluntary work with the police, an overwhelming 63 per cent indicated the enjoyment they received from the work. Some typical replies were:

Because I just love it – I just enjoy it.   (SC10)

I still enjoy doing it and I feel as though I am doing something. I must enjoy it to get home at 1.30 and up again at 6 o'clock. Also I feel wanted.   (SC48)

These replies are particularly striking since it is well recognized that most policework is mundane, although there is clearly a substantial difference between working full-time as an officer and being involved for only a few hours every week. The *potential* for excitement, for example, might be sufficient to maintain interest. Indeed, two sub-divisional officers we spoke to noted that it was easier to schedule specials for duty on a Friday or Saturday night when there was more street activity!

We shall be returning to these issues in Chapter 6. However, given the enthusiasm of specials for police work, it seems appropriate here to consider the attitudes of specials and regulars towards one another, starting with the views of regular officers.

POLICE OFFICERS' PERCEPTIONS OF SPECIALS

As we have noted above, whilst management and government policy may be favourably disposed towards the special constabulary, all the – admittedly impressionist – news from 'street' level is that the police are highly sceptical of the use of volunteers. Given police suspicion of outsiders in general (Holdaway 1983), this is not surprising; it is, however, interesting, given that, from the data cited above, police specials share many of the characteristics of regular officers.

In fact, only 7 per cent of our police respondents were female, confirming the over-representation of females amongst volunteers. The majority (82 per cent) were married. In terms of age, they fell into three roughly equal groups – those aged 30 or less, 31–40 and 41 or more, and were thus somewhat younger than both specials and probation officers. Although over two-thirds were constables, and only 9 per cent above the rank of sergeant, they had considerable experience of policing; only 15 per cent had less than six years' experience and nearly half had been in the police for at least 16 years. Three-quarters were working as uniformed officers and might therefore be expected to have the most contact with specials. In fact, three-quarters said that they did sometimes work with specials and over a third spent some off-duty time with them. While these figures are both lower than for the probation officers, we must remember that there are more volunteers for each paid employee in probation, thus accounting for much of the difference.

Asked what they felt were the aims of the special constabulary, respondents gave similar replies to the specials themselves, focusing on notions of back-up (especially in an emergency). Here the word 'assist' was used with almost monotonous regularity:

To assist the regular police but not to replace them.   (POL 002)

Assist where possible and on special occasions with the regular constabulary.   (POL 006)

To *assist* the regular police as a means of training for a time when they might be needed to replace regular police officers (i.e. state of emergency).   (POL 044)

Allied to this, and mentioned by a significant minority, was the notion of specials as representatives of the community contributing their local knowledge:

1. To provide a reserve of officers for special occasions or emergencies. 2. To act as eyes and ears for the police service. 3. To provide local knowledge (especially in rural areas).   (POL 001)

1. To provide a uniformed support for the regular officers. 2. To provide a link with the community. 3. To provide local knowledge.   (POL 045)

To provide a professional, voluntary back-up service to the regular force, and to provide a bridge between the police and the public.   (POL 203)

In marked contrast to probation officers, the police did not see volunteers as

TABLE 4.1 Police officers' perceptions of their relationships with special constables

	Very favour-able	Favour-able	In-different	Don't know	Un-favour-able	Very un-favour-able
	%	%	%	%	%	%
Personal attitudes towards specials	12	48	33	0	5	3
General attitudes of police towards specials	0	15	50	0	34	2
Specials' attitudes towards regulars	11	73	14	1	1	0

having any special qualities, other than the somewhat limited one of being able to provide information on their communities. Again in contrast, the emphasis was clearly on the special as a less capable assistant, someone to be called on when absolutely necessary, and a possible threat to one's overtime. During informal discussions this was repeated again and again, and many officers could think of no reasons why anyone would want to do policework for nothing! This was most evident when we asked the police what their personal views of specials were, and what they felt the police in general thought. As is clear from Table 4.1, on the first criterion, a majority said that they personally were favourably disposed towards specials, although a third were indifferent and some 8 per cent unfavourable. However, only 12 per cent felt that the officers in general were favourably disposed, with about half describing police attitudes as indifferent and over one-third as negative. On each of these criteria, replies were in marked contrast to those of probation officers. The general flavour of replies is given in the following quotes:

Having worked in a remote country station as a sole bobby, their experience and local knowledge was invaluable. (POL 085)

A valuable asset to officers in isolated areas where they undertake patrol duties with these officers. Relieve on traffic duties and social functions. (POL 007)

I do not consider them professional enough in the jobs of policing, but they are better than nothing at all. They are another uniform on the street and therefore carrying out a preventative role. (POL 113)

Specials perform a valuable function when engaged in parade type duties, when their involvement in actual policing is on a superficial level. That is, their involvement is in assisting rather than in dealing with theft etc. (POL 255)

Generally they are poorly trained and incompetent. Contrary to popular belief they would not have a clue how to do a regular's job and are merely there to make up numbers – being a body in uniform. (POL 024)

It takes two years of intense training, courses, examinations, practical experience and close monitoring to produce a competent officer able to deal fairly with all aspects of police duties. Even after this initial two years there are many things left to learn, usually by personal experience. An amateur cannot possibly hope to cover a fraction of this experience during his few hours training a week as a Special, even over many years.   (POL 246)

Perhaps the most significant word here is 'amateur'. To some of the police in our survey, specials were incompetent, perhaps even dangerous amateurs. To the majority they were well meaning, useful because of their community contacts, but not comparable with 'the real thing'. Ironically, while probation officers, with a widely recognized professional status, could identify numerous advantages in receiving help from those who were *not* professionals, the police, whose professional status is less well established, saw few advantages in the use of amateurs except as a last resort.[6] It is therefore particularly ironic, as also illustrated in Table 4.1, to find that the police very clearly identified specials as holding favourable views of *them*. In this context, it is thus appropriate to consider how those who volunteered to work with the police viewed the attitudes of those whom they wished to assist.

SPECIALS' PERCEPTIONS OF POLICE OFFICERS

The working environment within which specials carried out their voluntary policing, however, comprises not only policing activities, but also close contact with regular officers. As already noted, for example, most specials worked with regular officers, and contacts in the station or the police bar were a significant feature. However, the attitudes of regular officers to specials which we found, while supporting more impressionistic material from elsewhere, suggests that this environment would be anything but comfortable!

As with the probation service, we asked specials for their perceptions of their relationship with regulars, using an equivalent four questions. The answers are presented in Table 4.2. Like probation volunteers, specials felt that they themselves were viewed more favourably than other specials and that their views of the police were more positive than were those of other specials. Clearly, as regulars were aware, specials had extremely positive views of regular officers, but also felt that regulars were favourably inclined towards them, more so than is justified by the responses we received to the police questionnaire and indeed in conversations with regular officers.

What is clear is that specials were aware that some regulars were hostile, or at least 'anti-special'. One special, for example, recalled turning up for duty at his station and being asked by an officer why he was there. When he replied that it was to help, he was told in no uncertain terms, 'You are no assistance.' Specific examples like this tended to be accounted for in impersonal terms. The threat posed to regular officers' overtime was especially mentioned in this respect:

> I think they are anti. They believe we are taking duties from them when they could be paid overtime for taking those duties.   (SC06)

TABLE 4.2 Police specials' perceptions of their relationships with police officers

	Very favour-able	Favour-able	In-different	Don't know	Un-favour-able	Very un-favour-able
	%	%	%	%	%	%
Police attitudes towards them	48	44	8	0	2	0
Police attitudes towards specials in general	18	57	20	0	6	0
Own views of regulars with whom they worked	53	47	0	0	0	0
Views specials in general held about regulars	31	49	8	12	0	0

I think they think we are taking their overtime; that is the long and short of it. (SC44)

To counteract such criticism, respondents indicated that *they personally*, through their commitment and attitudes, had been able to prove themselves. Four specials can be cited to illustrate this:

Perhaps because I do more hours than most and therefore meet them more. (SC23)

Most of the regulars are great . . . anyway they prefer the more experienced special. They have to prove themselves. (SC48)

I get on with ninety-five percent of them because I don't push myself. If they ask me to do something I do it. If they don't I shut up. (SC07)

They seem friendly. We don't step on their toes. In fact we stand back and do what we are told. (SC10)

In one respect, this entailed remaining on the margins of police activity, acting as a general assistant to the regular. In other respects, however, it required proof of commitment to police values and proof that one could be depended upon. This was well illustrated during training weekends, when specials would inevitably gravitate to the police bar during the evening. Here specials were able to relate stories of experiences on the beat, or catch up on a police gossip (such as which regulars had been promoted). It was also where values could be transmitted: police jargon – such as 'feeling a collar', 'shout' and 'tour' became an integral part of the conversation. They helped to provide a sense of identity with the service.

Not surprisingly then specials were also seen to adopt police ways of dealing with incidents. In training sessions specials learned there was a difference between the theory and practice of police work. The formation of these ideas in class was reinforced in the bar. Car chases, but especially fights or any other

incident when there was a hint of rule bending, were always related enthusiastically to an appreciative audience. The following is but one example:

> I was out on one occasion with a group of officers, quite a few of us there were,
> when we came across a bunch of yobs. They were a bit hippy, and we realized
> we would have to do something about it. So, we began to argue (with them) a
> bit. Then one police constable, standing away from us all, bent over pretending
> to have been thumped. He hadn't of course, but we had so many statements
> saying he had been hit it was incredible. Anyway, we had the yobs, it was a
> good night.

The audience of specials applauded what they considered commendable police
work. The rules had been broken, but this was justifiable in order to detain
'yobs'. This story was told quite candidly and sparked off a sequence of similar
memories of instances where specials had been involved in 'real police work'. We
do need, however, to add an important comment to these stories. We do not wish
to suggest that specials sought pleasure in bending rules. Neither did officers, as
specials stressed in conversations with us. Our point is merely that where, in
police terms, rule breaking is defined as necessary to achieve objectives, specials
would be likely to concur. The extent to which they could act as public eyes
righting all the wrongs of police officers is then brought into question (Gill 1987).

That specials could always be available and help regulars was a sacrosanct
principle. Nearly always they did, and we heard stories of specials, off duty,
coming to the assistance of regulars. This was not always the case, however, as the
following dialogue indicates:

> *Special*: This regular was on duty when he got into a fight. Then he saw a
> special off duty in the crowd watching and so the regular called for
> help. The special didn't bloody move – did he? – the silly old sod
> wouldn't help out. Well you can imagine what we all thought can't
> you?
>
> *MG*: Well what did you think and did you find out?
>
> *Special*: How did we find out? Christ, every special rang every other special
> with the news, it was round the Division within an hour. The special
> concerned is an old guy. We all thought he would get the sack but it
> looks like he is just going to be carpeted for it.
>
> *MG*: What did the regulars think?
>
> *Special*: Well for those who don't like specials, you can imagine this was
> perfect ammunition. But the majority realized this was just one of
> those things that we all deplored. In fact the truth is the specials were
> more annoyed than the regulars. Anyway, about two weeks later (a
> week ago) we were redeemed when a special did help out in a tight
> spot. We really needed that lift – we are popular once again, but that
> old sod better never turn up again, we could well do without that
> type.

That specials should consider this issue so important is indicative of their level of commitment to police work. At the same time it shows that specials recognized the delicacy of their position: their acceptance by police officers depended on their illustrating their competence as assistants in policing and this was enshrined in specials' perspectives of their role alongside the regular.

Finally here, it is worth referring briefly to details from the questionnaire completed by 24 specials who resigned during the research period. We have included this material in more depth elsewhere (Gill and Mawby 1990). However, it is important to stress in the present context that there was no evidence of any disenchanted minority leaving the service with negative impressions of the work or their reception from regular officers. For example, 80 per cent described their experiences as either enjoyable or very enjoyable, all but one felt that specials were necessary, and only two said that their view of the police had changed for the worse. As many as 83 per cent said they had friends among the specials and a similar number had made friends with regular officers. Overall, it appears that volunteers resigned from the special constabulary because of circumstances unrelated to the voluntary work itself and remained committed to police work and the regular force.

SUMMARY

The special constabulary has changed in a number of respects in recent years. It has moved from being a unit for emergency use only to a highly structured supplement to day-to-day policing. Moreover, the voluntary principle has been underlined and has gained more explicit government approval within the last two or three years. For all this, there is very little research available on specials, and it is instructive to consider them in comparison with other groups of volunteers.

Clearly some of the findings on police volunteers are in marked contrast to those for probation. However, in many other respects the difference is largely one of emphasis. For example, while the average probation officer has a more positive perception of 'volunteering' than does the average police officer, he or she at least shares some of the concerns of the latter that volunteers introduce certain changes into the job, through unreliability or as a threat to one's work/overtime. In this context, comparison with victim-support volunteers, who operate with *both* agencies, is instructive.

Additionally, we have identified a number of differences in the ways in which probation and police volunteers approach their work with the agency. The latter more closely identify with 'police work' than more general 'voluntary work', for example, and prioritize the excitement elements which the work sometimes generates. This partly explains the very different types of volunteer entering the two agencies, and the consequentially different implications such issues raise for the organizations. Before considering these matters further, however, we turn to assess the role of volunteers in a different setting, with voluntary agencies working with crime victims.

5

VICTIM SUPPORT

HISTORICAL INTRODUCTION

Victim services of any sort are of recent origin. Indeed the literature is replete with introductions lamenting the absence, until very recently, of interest and concern for crime victims. In Britain, for example, some of the problems faced by victims may have been covered incidentally by statutory welfare services dealing with income maintenance, health, housing, or family relationships. However, these were in no way systematically expressed *vis-à-vis* crime victims, and indeed critiques of some of these services, for example, regarding violence within the home towards women and children, have focused on the inadequacy of provision.

In other respects services specifically directed at crime victims emerged in the 1960s with the introduction of the Criminal Injuries Compensation Board (CICB), whereby victims of injury from violent crime could apply for compensation from the state; where an offender was found guilty of violence or property crime, the 1972 Criminal Justice Act then allowed the court to impose a compensation order. A critique of these provisions and their subsequent modifications, is contained elsewhere (Mawby and Gill 1987, Chapters 3–4).

However, no state agencies appeared to accept any responsibilities for providing personal support, advice and comfort to crime victims. The emergence of the Bristol Victims Support Scheme, in 1973–4 (Holtom and Raynor 1988; Mawby and Gill 1987), and its development into a national movement can thus be seen as a twentieth-century equivalent to the nineteenth-century voluntary agencies which were formed to fill a vacuum of state inaction.

In fact, the voluntary principle was credited with considerable importance within victim support. Whilst a management committee was formed with representatives from a number of statutory agencies, most notably police and probation, and the key post of co-ordinator identified, the importance of victim support as an independent organization utilizing community resources and deploying volunteers was stressed. Services were to be provided by volunteers calling on victims within a day or two of the crimes coming to the attention of the police. Given the inexperience of volunteers it was decided to exclude more serious crimes of an interpersonal nature; because of the need to limit demand, crimes seen as less traumatic, like vehicle-related thefts, were also excluded and consequently burglaries became the most common crimes referred to and dealt with by schemes.

The Bristol scheme experienced a number of teething problems, but publicity on a BBC 'Open Door' programme and support from the National Association for the Care and Resettlement of Offenders (NACRO) helped maintain the initiative, and by the end of the 1970s there were some 67 schemes operating within a national body, the National Association of Victims Support Schemes (NAVSS) now called Victim Support. By March 1986 there were 293 schemes dealing with some 185,000 annual referrals and victim support had attained the status of one of the fastest growing areas of voluntary-sector provision.

THE INTERNATIONAL SCENE

Lack of response to the problems of crime victims was not specific to Britain. In the United States recommendations by the 1967 President's Commission on Law Enforcement and the Administration of Justice, concerned that a hostile criminal justice system was deterring victims and witnesses from co-operating in the prosecution process, led to a series of projects aimed at enhancing the role of victims and witnesses in the process. These initiatives were given impetus by a number of academics and practitioners who organized the First International Symposium on Victimology in Israel in 1974. Partly flowing from this initiative, the National Organization for Victim Assistance (NOVA) was formed as an umbrella organization, and during the mid- to late 1970s it expanded to serve as a national clearing house of information and as co-ordinator for victim-service programmes including Rape Crisis Centers, Victim/Witness Assistance Programs, Spouse Abuse Centers, Parents of Murdered Children, and Mothers Against Drunk Driving, a series of initiatives which we have described in more detail elsewhere (Mawby and Gill 1987, Chapter 7).

As is evident from the above list, however, whilst such schemes emerged at a similar time to victim support in Britain, they were markedly different in a number of respects, not surprising when one considers that NAVSS and NOVA were apparently unaware of each other's existence until 1982 (Pointing and Maguire 1988). Thus help for victims in the United States has most commonly adopted a rights- rather than a needs-based approach (Simon 1987); focused on victims of violent crime and sexual assault; placed more emphasis on either immediate response to the scene of the crime (Bolin 1980) or communication by telephone; prioritized help for victims in court (Schneider and Schneider 1981);

and placed emphasis on the long-term traumas faced by crime victims and the consequent importance of professional help (Young and Stein 1983). It has thus been less influenced by the voluntary principle.

In Canada, where services emerged somewhat later, a similar pattern is evident, although volunteers are a more central feature of services in areas where British traditions are still influential, less so in Quebec Province. As in the United States, however, victims' rights are prioritized and services are more closely allied to statutory agencies, especially the police, rather than being independent (Rock 1988; Waller 1988). McClenahan (1987), for example, describes the work of the Victim/Witness Service Unit in Vancouver. The unit, based in police departments, provides a rapid response service to crime victims through 140 volunteers.

Services in other countries, notably Western Europe and Australia, are described – albeit briefly – elsewhere (Van Dijk 1985, 1988; Vidosa 1988; Waller 1988). Thus in the Netherlands, while some of the early schemes focused on domestic violence victims, help for victims of property crime, as in the UK, is now more common. Nevertheless, as in the USA initial contact is commonly by telephone. There are currently over 50 local schemes, co-ordinated through a national organization, with over 500 volunteers; many are run on similar lines to those in the UK, but some work closely with, or are administered by, state agencies including social-work departments. In South Australia, victim services are handled within autonomous agencies and depend on volunteers, as in Britain, but appear to have adopted a rights-based approach more synonymous with the North American model.[1]

While victim services have emerged in a number of countries, their precise forms vary markedly – for example, in terms of the victims of crimes with which they deal, their use of volunteers, their relationship with statutory agencies, and their underpinning ideologies. To a lesser extent, however, similar variations are evident between services within a single country, such as the UK, where traditional semi-autonomous developments combine with recent initiatives based on ideas from home and abroad to provide a wealth of diversity.

THE NATIONAL PICTURE

By the end of 1987 there were some 360 schemes and districts affiliated to the NAVSS in England and Wales, and similar developments in Scotland and Northern Ireland (NAVSS 1988). A measure of uniformity is enforced through the constitution and schemes are only affiliated if they fulfil certain requirements regarding management-committee representation, volunteer training, etc. The linchpin of every scheme is the co-ordinator who is responsible for ensuring that referrals are received from the police and for allocating visits to the volunteers (Maguire and Corbett 1987). Originally most co-ordinators were themselves volunteers. However, gradually co-ordinators tended to receive some funding, sometimes an honorarium, perhaps by the assignment of a part- or full-time post. At first such posts were funded through government work-creation programmes like Urban Aid, the Inner City Partnership or MSC funding. However in 1986 the government made money available nationally for the NAVSS to allocate funds to local schemes considered in need of immediate financial support, and in late 1987 it announced a £9 million package of funding over the three-year period 1988–91, the bulk to be used for the payment of full-time local co-ordinators. It is currently envisaged that at least one full-time co-ordinator per scheme will become the norm. Concomitant with this funding initiative, the local structure of victim support has changed such that individual schemes are now grouped within a county rather than a regional structure. There has also been a recent move to standardize the names of local schemes and simplify that of the national organization.

National statistics also reveal one further gradual change, a shift away from the traditional focus on burglary victims. Thus, while NAVSS (1988) figures for 1986–7 show that 72 per cent of referrals were for burglary, this reflects a decline from 80 per cent in 1984–5. At the same time victim-support schemes dealt with approximately 300 homicides, 900 rapes, 20,000 robberies and 22,000 woundings and assaults[2] and in all the cases of robberies the percentage of victims known to the police who were referred to schemes is greater than for household burglaries. There is, however, a marked variation between schemes in this respect. While some schemes have maintained their concentration upon burglary victims, a number, encouraged by the National Association and other agencies (such as the police), have devoted more attention to serious crimes like homicide and especially rape (Corbett and Hobdell 1988), and as a result have prioritized the need for specialist intensive training for volunteers. Not surprisingly, schemes in Northern Ireland also cover a range of serious offences (McLachlan 1988). Response to social harassment has also been a subject of debate (Cooper and Pomeyie 1988). At the other extreme, many schemes are willing to visit victims of non-criminal incidents referred to them by police or other agencies, including traffic accidents and fire casualties.[3]

The variation in incidents covered by schemes is just one illustration of the different practices operated both between and within areas. Here it is perhaps most appropriate to consider three more: workload; referral policies; and service. In considering the national picture for probation and police volunteers we have already identified the problem of inequitable distribution. A similar problem emerges for victim support. As we have detailed elsewhere, whereas schemes were initiated throughout the country, considerable variations in workload exist due to the difficulty of attracting volunteers in high-crime metropolitan areas where referrals are consequently prolific (Mawby and Gill 1987). A sample of 72 schemes in 1984, for example, ranged from some with less than four referrals per volunteer per *year* to those with over four referrals per volunteer per *week*. Thus whilst some schemes suffer from the problem of overworked volunteers with consequent burnout, others confront poor volunteer morale due to underuse.

The problem of a mismatch between volunteer resources and service demand is endemic to the voluntary sector, and an issue we highlighted in Chapter 2. It is therefore instructive to assess how victim support has attempted to alleviate the problem. One way is through the injection of funds into areas where needs are greatest. In deciding which schemes should be funded for full-time co-ordinators, this was clearly a factor to which the NAVSS accredited importance. Similarly, in some areas where schemes had not developed 'spontaneously' co-ordinators have been appointed to *initiate* schemes. The Prescot VSS is a case in point.[4] Third, at least one scheme, in Birmingham, has required MSC funding to employ those involved in visiting crime victims.[5]

A final means of addressing the problem of over-demand, common to both voluntary and statutory welfare services (Foster 1983), is through the rationing of the service provided. That is, whilst in semi-rural schemes with low numbers of referrals it is common practice for all referrals to receive a visit, in hard-pressed areas co-ordinators may act as gatekeepers and decide which victims receive a visit and how to respond to the remainder. Nationally, in 1986–7, only some 39 per cent of referrals resulted in a personal visit with 33 per cent contacted by letter and 7 per cent by phone (NAVSS 1988). However, as Maguire and Corbett (1987) detail for an earlier period, such an overall picture hides considerable local variation, with some schemes able to visit personally most referrals and some more dependent on communication by letter or telephone.

The workload of individual schemes has been markedly affected by changing referral practices. Originally schemes depended on the police for referrals. However, while self-referrals are relatively uncommon – in 1986–7, for example, police referrals accounted for 96 per cent of the total (NAVSS 1988) – decisions over which victims of which crimes the police referred to schemes have been subject to much controversy. The situation where the police make that decision has been undermined by critiques of police gatekeeping whereby only the stereotypical vulnerable victim (the little old lady living alone) might be referred for help (Maguire and Corbett 1987; Mawby and Gill 1987). As a result of such concerns, NAVSS policy, now widely adopted by police forces, is for direct referrals, with all crimes in predetermined categories being referred to victim support and a decision then taken within the scheme, usually by the co-ordinator, as to the appropriate response. However, while a majority of schemes now operate a direct referral system, a number do not. Moreover, as indicated above, this change does not necessarily eliminate problems associated with gatekeeping but merely shifts its location; instead of the police deciding which victims are in need of a visit from a volunteer, schemes themselves are more likely to make that decision. Such a shift is not, unfortunately, a guarantee that all those in need will receive support, especially where resources are strained.

Finally it is important to reconsider the services provided to help crime victims. In most cases this involves visiting victims within one or two days of the crime and providing comfort, advice and a 'listening ear'; help with making claims for insurance or to the CICB or with arranging for repairs to be carried out is also common. Most of those visited, however, receive only one visit;

Maguire and Corbett (1987) suggest that this applies in three-quarters of cases. However, schemes with fewer referrals may emphasize repeat visits, and as other schemes have become involved with more serious crimes including sexual offences or violence, then a series of visits may be necessary, both to help the victim through a period of difficult readjustment and to provide support through the problems of appearing in court, giving evidence, etc. This in turn has provoked victim support to look more closely at the needs of victims in court, and a recent working party (Ralphs 1988) has made recommendations *vis-à-vis* both changes to court practices and changes in the type of work carried out by volunteers. Indicative of this, some schemes, including Guildford and North Tyneside and Blyth Valley[6] have recently promoted initiatives whereby volunteers have been assigned to help victims in court. The different demands of such work and the different requirements for volunteers' time raise the question of whether different sorts of volunteer may be available and/or suitable for different types of work with victims. Allied to the trend, noted above, for more concentrated work with victims of very serious offences, it may well be that in the future victim-support schemes will shift towards the recruitment of different volunteers for different tasks.

Variations in the operation of different schemes are therefore marked. As we have stressed elsewhere (Mawby and Gill 1987) the first schemes to be established tended to be in either high-crime urban areas *or* in less densely populated areas where crime posed less of a problem but volunteers were plentiful. Changes in recent years within victim support have tended to accentuate these 'ideal types'. Thus a number of the metropolitan schemes, struggling under heavy workloads, have taken on more cases, and more demanding cases, and looked for ways of funding back-up support. In contrast, many semi-rural schemes have been able to meet demand without much difficulty and have therefore become comfortable in providing a traditional service, reacting with suspicion to advice from central office and seeing any move towards a dependence on paid staff as heresy. It is important to stress this point here, because as we move on to concentrate on schemes in the Devon and Cornwall area we must be fully aware of how far they differ from, or reflect, the national pattern.

VICTIM SUPPORT IN DEVON AND CORNWALL

The relatively early emergence of victim support in the two counties owed much to the proximity of Bristol. Indeed initially they were all part of the same 'South West' region. By 1978 schemes were operating in Exeter, Plymouth, Barnstaple and Torbay and the first Cornwall scheme was opened in Camborne and Redruth shortly afterwards. By the time of our research, 14 schemes existed, 12 of which were incorporated in the study. When the county structure replaced the regions in 1988, there were 10 schemes operating in Devon and 11 in Cornwall. However only in Plymouth, where the scheme had experienced a variety of difficulties (Mawby and Gill 1987), was there a full-time paid co-ordinator, and some local schemes were indeed critical of such developments which they saw as a corruption of the voluntary principle.

The number of referrals made to schemes in the South-west was well below the national average, partly as a result of low crime rates and the fact that schemes covered relatively small areas, partly due to problems with police referrals which we have discussed in detail elsewhere (Mawby and Gill 1987). As a result, the ratio of referrals to volunteers was generally low, and in the context of the previous section Devon and Cornwall schemes were clearly among those in which volunteers were an under-used resource.

This had at least three implications for the operation of schemes and the work carried out by volunteers. First, since gatekeeping decisions were commonly made by the police, a very large majority of those who were referred were visited; contact by telephone or letter was less common except where no one was at home when a personal visit was made. Second, a number of local schemes were able and willing to widen their role to include non-crime victims, in cases of fire or road accidents, for example, and indeed in one scheme work with elderly *offenders* was incorporated at one time. Finally, compared with the national picture described by Maguire and Corbett (1987), we found a greater use of follow-up visits.

In other respects, however, the local pattern conformed to that nationally. Management committees incorporated a range of agency representatives, with probation and especially police playing a major part; pressures of day-to-day management of schemes fell heavily on the shoulders of co-ordinators. Volunteer training was a significant feature, taking place on average over six weeks and consolidated after that through volunteer meetings; and volunteers provided a quick response service to victims, especially of burglary, in which sympathy and support were key features (Mawby and Gill 1987). In contrast, it was in terms of characteristics of the volunteers themselves that schemes in the area were most distinctive.

THE VOLUNTEERS

In comparison with probation and police, the recruitment of volunteers by victim-support schemes is fundamentally distinct in at least two respects. On the one hand, since the movement is relatively new, established practices of recruitment are absent and the service is less well known to possible volunteers. On the other hand, the fact that services are based in local voluntary agencies adds an additional tendency towards variations in the practice of recruitment.

To an even greater extent than elsewhere volunteers with victim support, hearing about the service from acquaintances, drifted into a particular scheme. There were, of course exceptions: some applied on the basis of press articles, some were trawled from other voluntary agencies or volunteer bureaux. But commonly schemes relied on word of mouth.

In this context, the significant question becomes 'whose mouth?' In fact, we found that it was common practice for volunteers or management-committee members to suggest contacts as potential new volunteers, these follow-ups resulting in adequate numbers to cover referrals. In the specific context of the South-west then, certain social groups may predominate in victim support. More generally we might suggest that, where recruiting sufficient volunteers is not difficult and such methods are used, homogeneity of *some* sort among volunteers is likely.

In Devon and Cornwall, as we have detailed elsewhere (Mawby and Gill 1987), the results of this process were striking. Thus, whilst 59 per cent of volunteers were female and a large majority were married, data on socio-economic status and age were most notable. Most were middle class, with 62 per cent in social classes I and II and 2 per cent in social classes IV and V, and the unemployed were significant in their absence. One-third had experienced higher education and a further 22 per cent had pursued post-secondary education, again underlining the status division. However, only 47 per cent were currently employed, with 18 per cent classified as housewives and a third retired, a reflection of the age profile of these volunteers. Indeed half of those interviewed were aged over 55, with nearly one-third aged over 60. Not surprisingly, then, while 90 per cent had children, two-thirds of these were over the compulsory schooling age.

The high socio-economic status of our sample is notable, even in the context of other studies of volunteers. Moreover, victim-support volunteers in the South-west also appear relatively old compared with others, the exception being agencies specializing in services for the elderly (Hadley and Scott 1980). The differences between these and volunteers working in probation and the police force will be stressed in the following chapter. Here it is perhaps most useful to emphasize the fact that such findings, while perhaps not typical of victim support nationally, may be indicative of the grass-roots movement outside the metro-politan areas and where recruitment is not a significant problem. If, as was suggested earlier, victims' services are in the process of fundamental change, schemes in the South-west may well typify the 'old guard', becoming more of a minority but unlikely to 'fade away'.

Indeed the strength of commitment to victim support among volunteers in the South-west is well illustrated if we consider why volunteers became involved in voluntary work in general, and specifically in victim support. Asked why they had originally undertaken voluntary work, 40 per cent gave answers we classified as self-directed, 18 per cent other-directed reasons and 16 per cent could be said to have drifted into voluntary work. Somewhat fewer gave religious-based reasons (13 per cent) or claimed a specific interest in the agency or organization (9 per cent) and only one person had viewed voluntary work as a step towards a career.

Asked why they had joined victim support, 40 per cent registered an agency interest, but a majority (57 per cent) were classified as having drifted into this area of work. As we have noted elsewhere (Mawby and Gill 1987), this notion of drift was particularly relevant as a reaction to suggestions made to respondents. Victim-support schemes seeking volunteers would commonly ask around for 'suitable' volunteers, and those who joined 'just happened' to have time on their hands when the suggestion was made. For example:

> I was asked to do it, I didn't know about it till then.   (VS 21)

> A local policeman came to see me and said, 'Do you think it would be a good idea?' So I said, 'Yes', and that was it.   (VS 45)

Others drifted into the work either because of their contact through another agency, because they were directed by a volunteer bureau, or because the opportunity arose at the right moment. To give one example:

> I went to X Volunteer Services Bureau. They recommended I come, so I thought OK.   (VS 24)

Of those who were coded as having agency-directed reasons, most gave answers which demonstrated a concern for victims specifically. For example:

> I used to be a voluntary associate and so always thought so much was done for the offender and I wanted to help the victim.   (VS 50)

In fact, replies to a later question gave rather more support to this agency-led focus. Thus, when asked whether they had been motivated more by an interest in work with victims or towards voluntary work in general, 49 per cent claimed a victim-specific interest, 46 per cent a more general motivation.

Volunteers' reasons for continuing with their work with victim support were, however, somewhat different. In direct contrast to police specials, only 15 per cent explicitly stated that the work was enjoyable in itself. Rather more (27 per cent) gave altruistic or other-directed reasons and 6 per cent cited their religious convictions. Most notably, though, 26 per cent answered in ways we categorized as agency-led. For example:

> Oh, I think it is an active organization and I think the need will increase.   (VS 34)

A further 14 per cent were coded as 'stickability', that is those who said that they would not give up something to which they had made a commitment:

> I've only just started anyway. I tend to stick with things when I take them up.   (VS 23)

Many of the local agencies were relatively new, and overall victim support was struggling to establish itself. The result was the reinforcement of a sense of commitment among volunteers. Despite their under-use, volunteers felt that schemes were necessary and saw their continued involvement as crucial, if crime victims were to receive the help they deserved. Although in many cases morale was low, this was consequently seen as a reason for *persevering*, not quitting.

Like probation volunteers, volunteers in victim support commonly operated in relative isolation from other volunteers, a fact accentuated by the lack of an agency base, in any physical sense, and lack of work. However, they shared with police specials a commitment, in this case to a client group which needed them. Victim support thus became the symbol, the cause to which volunteers could adhere.

PROFESSIONALS' PERCEPTIONS OF VOLUNTEERS

Unlike the police and probation fields, where some sort of relationship between some full-time employees and some volunteers is inevitable, victim-support schemes are autonomous units within which volunteers may operate without any direct contact with *any* paid employees. This is, of course, decreasingly the case as more and more schemes appoint paid co-ordinators, and indeed the extent to which co-ordinator–visitor relationships differ between schemes with a paid officer and those with a volunteer co-ordinator is an interesting but unresearched issue. Equally, where a scheme employs paid visitors, the relationship between these and longstanding volunteer visitors is one of potential conflict. However, in Devon and Cornwall, as already noted, there is currently only one paid co-ordinator; the key relationship of relevance here is thus with employees of other agencies which impinge on victim support.

These are largely reflected in presence on the management committee of a scheme and/or contact during day-to-day operations. In each context the two agencies most directly involved are police and probation, the former more especially, given their status as initial gatekeepers of referrals. Within the British system, as Shapland (1988) points out, such agencies may be regarded as 'fiefs', maintaining their own independent perspective but having a significant impact on the operation of victim services.

Our postal questionnaires to police and probation officers focused on respondents' views of both volunteers within their own agencies *and* victim support. On this level one general point requires expression. In each case professionals were very positive about both the need for victim support and its appropriate place in the voluntary sector. In the case of the police especially the voluntary nature of victim support received a more positive response than did the availability of a special constabulary! Overall then, professionals accepted the need for victim support and saw advantages in its independence, both in terms of political balance as a separate 'fief' and as a response to those who might criticize their own agencies for avoiding victims' needs.

That said, however, clearly the response of the police is of more significance and in this respect we highlighted three further issues (Mawby and Gill 1987: Chapter 9). First, on a management level the police had responded extremely positively to the development of victim services in the force area. Senior police officers had been active in initiating schemes and, as our observational work illustrated, were extremely prominent on management committees. Second, the potential for co-operation was enhanced by the very positive attitudes of volunteers towards the police; indeed in this respect victim-support-scheme volunteers' views were very similar to those of special constables. Third, however, we found that in a number of schemes low referral rates were causing several problems, a fact which we attributed to both the lack of awareness among many police of the precise service provided by schemes and most especially an underestimation by the police of the needs of crime victims in general. In arguing that schemes need both to enlarge their profile at ground level and to increase their power (by controlling referrals), we would thus stress that the volunteer–professional relationship can be as crucial within voluntary agencies as it is within statutory bodies which deploy volunteers.

VOLUNTEERS' ATTITUDES TOWARDS POLICE AND PROBATION

We have already suggested that victim-support volunteers displayed a high regard for the police, a point we shall reconsider in a wider context in the next chapter. At the same time, and given the focus of the probation service on offenders, we shall discuss the perspectives of victim-support volunteers towards offenders and sentencing alternatives. However, at this point we wish to make some brief comments on the need for police and probation involvement with victim support, according to those volunteers who were working (or about to work) with victims.

The need for police involvement on the committee of victim support was hardly questioned by volunteers. In all, 91 per cent considered police involvement *necessary*. Perhaps not surprisingly the main reason offered focused on the role of police as referrers. Nevertheless, some commented that police training and experience were themselves of value to volunteers. These points were reiterated by the co-ordinators we spoke to who had a high regard and good working relationship with officers. This was despite, in some cases, a belief that not all possible referrals were arriving at victim support. For most volunteers and co-ordinators referral problems were the major source of criticism of the police. However, there was a small minority of volunteers which considered that the work of victim support was distinct from that of policing.

The balance of views on the appropriateness of probation involvement was somewhat different. When asked about the need for probation-service representation on management committees, only just over half our respondents felt that this was *necessary*. Nevertheless very few were actually hostile towards the probation service, with rather more feeling that the focus of their organization on the *victim* by definition excluded an *offender*-oriented organization. Moreover, some who considered that probation involvement was not *necessary* still judged it *preferable*. Reasons given for maintaining probation involvement centred on three points: that probation officers' knowledge and experience were relevant, not least with respect to the 'other side of the coin', the offender; that probation had demonstrated commitment to victim support over a long period; and that where officers were involved their contribution had been appreciated. In all then, volunteers displayed a favourable attitude towards the involvement of both probation and especially police in their organization, reaffirming one of the founding principles of victim support.

SUMMARY

In all it can be seen that notions of the forgotten crime victim now seem less appropriate both in Britain and abroad. The expansion in services since the 1960s has been considerable, the CICB was followed by compensation orders, ameliorating the financial losses of crime, and victim-support schemes followed, offering emotional, practical and advisory assistance. While initially schemes tended to be formed in high-crime conurbations or more rural good volunteer areas, today they cover nearly all parts of the British Isles.

During this period, and inevitably, changes have taken place: for example, more victims are helped and there is greater police acceptance of the need for victim support. Some changes have, however, received a mixed reception. A case in point is the greater dependence on paid posts that expansion has necessitated, and the resulting central-government funding. Some schemes have seen this as a move away from the much valued voluntary principle.

In many important respects, though, the original principles of victim support are intact. Schemes are still operated through a committee of local representatives; help tends to be short term; referrals are received by the co-ordinator; and most helpers are still volunteers.

Given that volunteers with victim support work within a voluntary agency, rather than a statutory one, the issues raised in this chapter are slightly different from the preceding ones, and even where some similar issues are discussed, for example, volunteer–professional relationships, the context is markedly different. The question of who volunteers, and why, is just as crucial a one, yet despite Smith's (1985) interesting discussion paper, there is little published data available except for our own. Yet here parallels and contrasts with the material on police and probation volunteers are most evident. Thus, in their social characteristics, victim-support volunteers were very similar to probation volunteers. However in their motivation for choosing to work with victim support, and in their reasons for continuing such work, they were distinctive, emphasizing the contrasting characteristics of victim-support schemes, in terms of both organizational and ideological features. These issues become the focus of the following two chapters.

6

TOWARDS AN IDEOLOGY OF VOLUNTEERING

INTRODUCTION

Despite the range of studies on volunteers and volunteering, and the many similarities in findings, very little attention has been directed at examining the lessons that can be heeded. This is in part due to a focus on the organization rather than the individual, and on the professional rather than the volunteer. It is also fuelled by the difficulty in locating studies; too many have not yet been published and remain in-house reports. In this chapter we hope, at least in part, to rectify that deficiency by drawing on our own research findings. We aim to show that it is possible to theorize about voluntary activity; to discern key features of volunteering which agencies can influence to induce commitment, and consequently to maximize the volunteer's potential. It appears to us essential to consider the very nature of volunteering as a stepping stone to formulating policies designed to increase the role of the community. It is this failure to do so previously which has resulted in an incredible under-utilization and even abuse of willing lay helpers. This theme is continued in Chapter 7. Here, however, we wish to stress that such practical issues have a direct theoretical relevance, particularly regarding volunteer ideologies. We shall start by considering what we have termed 'the volunteer process', illustrated in Figure 6.1.

The flow chart seeks to show the various decisions which may be made by either the volunteer or the organization from initial attraction to voluntary work to continuance with, or resignation from it. Assessing these various decisions for our samples, enables a comparison of the ways in which influences are or can be generated. Essentially we are concerned with identifying similarities and differences and at the same time seeking explanations for them.

Thus, while on the one hand we see the 'volunteer process' as a way of discussing our findings, and structuring this chapter, we do none the less

FIGURE 6.1   The volunteer process: a decision-making model

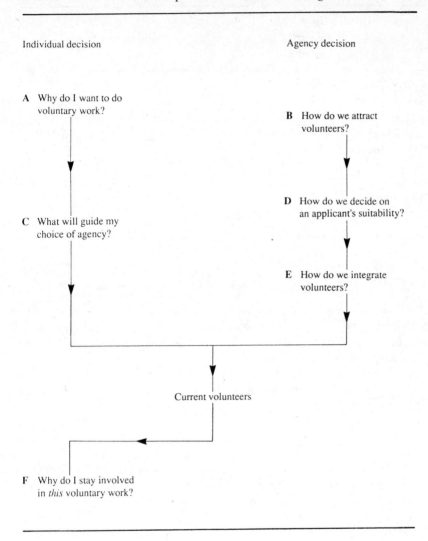

Individual decision

Agency decision

A Why do I want to do
voluntary work?

B How do we attract
volunteers?

C What will guide my
choice of agency?

D How do we decide on
an applicant's suitability?

E How do we integrate
volunteers?

Current volunteers

F Why do I stay involved
in *this* voluntary work?

recognize that it will be a simplification. For example, while decisions A and C
are separated in the diagram we have already noted for specials in particular that
the reasons for wanting to do voluntary work may be synonymous with wanting
to work for a particular agency. At the same time it would be fatuous to believe
that all these decisions are always made, especially sequentially, a point to which
we shall return. First, however, we focus on the decisions taken, first by the
individual, then the agencies.

TABLE 6.1 Primary reason for becoming involved in voluntary work

	Probation volunteers n = 58	Police specials n = 51	VSS volunteers n = 55	Total n = 164
	%	%	%	%
Self-directed	26	43	40	36
Career	23	4	2	10
Agency-led	10	20	9	13
Other-directed	19	14	18	17
Religious	2	0	13	5
Drift	19	18	16	18
Don't know	0	2	2	1
Total	99	101	100	100

INDIVIDUAL DECISIONS

Most previous researchers have not distinguished between a volunteer's reason for undertaking voluntary work and the reason for joining a particular agency. Treating these two decisions as separate generated some interesting finds which are shown in Tables 6.1 and 6.2.

No less than two-fifths of specials and victim-support volunteers claimed to have initially volunteered for gains accruing to themselves; in our terminology they were 'self-directed'. Probation volunteers in contrast seemed to emphasize self-directed reasons less, except in the specific context of career aspirations. Essentially, if people volunteer for career aims, they are clearly volunteering for personal gains; hence career reasons are a specific form of self-directed reasoning. A caveat is necessary here though: it is possible to argue that, because people in their career choice want to help others, they are in fact volunteering for 'other-directed reasons'. In our view this argument is misconceived, partly because jobs involve payment and thus become divorced from conceptions of philanthropy, and partly because it ignores a host of factors concerning job availability. If it is legitimate to combine self-directed and career motivations as we have suggested, differences between the agencies are small. Indeed, given the size of the samples, they are remarkably similar.[1]

Another main difference between the samples is their relative emphasis on organizational or agency-led reasons. Earlier it was suggested that the decision to undertake voluntary work was separated from reasons for joining a particular agency. However, for those whose decisions were primarily agency led they were inseparable. In other words, individuals were attracted to becoming volunteers with a particular agency. This was especially the case with specials who in nearly a fifth of cases were attracted to police work, reflecting the distinctive nature of the special constabulary. It would have been surprising had the organization been important for victim support because it was so new at that time and many people would have been unsure as to precisely what volunteers do (Hough and Mayhew 1985). In any event the probation service and the victim support represent just two types of caring work (Samaritans and Marriage Guidance are others). The special constabulary, even with the advent of neighbourhood watch and moves to expand the Territorial Army, remains unique.

One other difference between the samples requires comment; that is the emphasis placed on religious motivations by victim-support volunteers. Given the inevitable link between religion and charitable work, we did ask our respondents questions about their religious beliefs. Here, victim-support volunteers were more likely than both specials and probation volunteers to attend a place of religious worship and, of those who did not, significantly more victim-support volunteers claimed they did hold religious beliefs. What does need to be remembered here though is that victim-support schemes frequently contained religious representatives on committees.[2] Given the word-of-mouth recruitment strategies, the pattern thus makes sense. Overall, though, it seems that without a specific religious involvement, most who volunteer will not be *primarily* motivated by religious reasons. In fact, and perhaps surprisingly, what is most striking about the initial decision to volunteer is the degree of similarity. Particularly interesting here is the prominence of what we have termed 'drift'. The drift effect has been largely ignored by previous researchers, although it is probably not a surprising finding. After all, if, as we suggest, most volunteers are recruited by word of mouth, then it is surely reasonable to assume that some will volunteer because they happened to be asked, rather than having any more specific reason. Moreover, our findings suggest that the drift effect is a characteristic of voluntary work generally (or perhaps of those agencies that rely on word of mouth as a main recruitment tool?) rather than being agency specific.

Finally, there are those whose primary reason we have defined as 'other-directed'. The specials were slightly less likely to volunteer for other-directed reasons, although the 'other' in question varies. For probation volunteers and victim support, other-directed reasons related more to wanting to help individuals, while specials were more likely to see the community as the main 'other', especially through the channel of maintaining law and order. Of course, this is interlinked with the type of agencies they chose, where the probation service and victim support focus on services for individuals, whereas the public helped by the special constabulary is both wider and vaguer.

If we include career reasons with the self-directed, then the major differences between the samples relate to agency-led and religious-based reasoning. Although we are working with small numbers, the results do encourage us to make some general comments about the initial decision to volunteer, at least for these three agencies in the criminal justice system.

Somewhere between a sixth and a fifth of our three samples combined did not make a predetermined decision to volunteer but drifted into voluntary work. A similar proportion, but slightly less for the specials, volunteer because of a desire to help others, either individuals or the community. However, over twice as many claimed to be initially motivated by career aspirations or other self-directed reasons.[3]

It has been noted that specials were more likely to emphasize organizational reasons, and we suggested that this was because of the uniqueness of the specials' role. By the same token we would expect other agencies like the Territorial Army to contain a large percentage of volunteers who are attracted by what we have termed organizational reasons. Similarly, we would contend that religion is in most cases unlikely to be a primary motivator. The exception will be where organizations are closely allied to the church/chapels or else recruit through a place of religious worship.

These exceptions here are important. It is suggested that all other things being equal, there are 'more permanent' and 'more variable' factors in the initial decision to volunteer. We present this information derived from the agencies in this study diagrammatically in Figure 6.2. It must be stressed that it is based on

FIGURE 6.2   Permanent and variable factors in primary reasons for volunteering

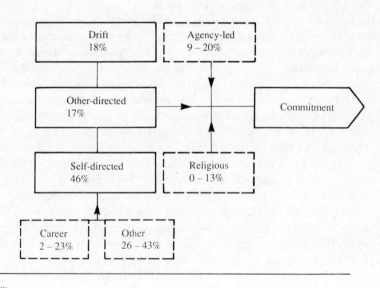

Key

☐ Permanent factor

⌐ ⌐ ⌐ Variable factor

our research (and the lack of others), but, if we are correct, then it marks a new point in our understanding of the primary reasons behind individuals' commitment to voluntary work.

Why, then, did individuals choose to work with a particular agency, in this case police, probation or victim support? The primary reasons cited in answer to our open-ended question are categorized in Table 6.2.

In the case of specials and victim-support volunteers, over 90 per cent of responses could be classified into two categories, 'drift' or 'a specific interest in the organization'. However, the relative prominence of these two varied. For specials the interest in the organization previously identified is underlined here. In contrast, victim-support volunteers tended to drift into the agency, although a large minority stated an interest in the organization, significant, given, as already noted, its recency. Indeed, it appears that the very fact that victim support was a new cause focusing on a previously unrecognized area encouraged involvement.

Probation volunteers were slightly different. True, these same two categories were prominent, but while the organization was the primary attraction, and well over a quarter drifted into voluntary probation work, a significant minority were primarily attracted to the probation service because of career interests. When these thirteen responses were analysed further, no less than ten also mentioned an interest in the probation service. The role of the organization as an attraction to volunteers is again highlighted,[4] and, if career and agency-led reasons are combined, probation and police contrast markedly with the newer, and less readily identified, victim-support movement.

This does beg the question of what precisely *is* the interest in the organization? After all, criminologists have tended to see victim and offender as quite different actors in the criminal justice system. Are then those who seek to help victims and those who seek to help offenders different types of people? Moreover, probation

TABLE 6.2 Primary reason for becoming involved in the specific form of voluntary work

	Probation volunteers n = 57	Police specials n = 51	VSS volunteers n = 53	Total n = 161
	%	%	%	%
Self-directed	5	0	0	2
Career	23	2	2	9
Agency-led	37	59	40	43
Other-directed	7	8	2	6
Drift	28	31	56	39
Total	100	100	100	99

officers tend to see offenders as people with problems, somewhat in contrast to police perceptions, perhaps best illustrated in the context of police and social-work perceptions of each other (Holdaway 1986). If we translate these differences to a political or ideological level, the police are certainly associated with the political right to an extent which the probation service is not. Nor for that matter is victim support (at least not in this country, see Mawby and Gill 1987) which has emerged with a mixture of both police and probation influence. Are these ideological differences transferable to volunteers? Put simply, can we assume that a person who believes in capital and corporal punishment would not join or would be less likely to join the probation service as a volunteer than the specials or victim support? Are there similar types of people in each of the organizations with similar views, reflecting the ideology of the agency?

Our results reported here lend only partial support to this hypothesis. While most volunteers mentioned an interest in the organization, it is not axiomatic that this interest can be interpreted as sharing an ideological perspective. In any event some drift into the work, perhaps persuaded by a similar type of person (with similar views?) or through some awareness of what they were drifting into. However, there was no relationship between reasons for undertaking voluntary work or joining a particular agency and any other variable. This suggests one of two things: either the ideology of the organization is unimportant, or that the organization can have an effect on all, or most, individuals, no matter why they joined. The influence of the agency is much broader than this, however.

AGENCY DECISIONS

It has long been established that volunteers tend to be recruited by informal methods such as word of mouth (Aves 1969; Humble 1982; H. Jackson 1985) and our findings, perhaps not surprisingly, provide support for this. However, rather less has been said of the implications. We have already mentioned the relevance of the drift effect in people being involved incidentally (when asked), rather than making a predetermined decision to volunteer. Later, we shall illustrate the consequences of word-of-mouth recruiting in involving the same type of people. At the same time, though, other methods were used.

When volunteers were in short supply, agencies did advertise. This was especially the case with the special constabulary, where local television campaigns have spearheaded recruitment initiatives. At the same time some victim-support schemes have advertised in the press, and along with specials in one sub-division have benefited from stalls and displays at local events, serving the dual function of advertising and recruiting. Similarly one senior probation officer, newly appointed, advertised in the press to initiate a volunteer group. Moreover, some probation volunteers were prompted to join the probation service following a talk by a probation officer. Agencies may additionally encourage referrals from volunteer bureaux, although this appeared rare as far as the agencies we covered were concerned.

In all then, we can say that word of mouth predominated, but that agencies were prepared to resort to more formal methods when either more or specific types of volunteers were required. So who then was considered an acceptable applicant?

There were intra- as well as inter-agency differences in the means by which each agency decided on the acceptability of volunteers. Notwithstanding this, the specials were particularly distinctive with a highly structured process, in contrast to the probation service and the largely informal arrangement in victim-support schemes where informality was linked to knowing the people concerned.

The distinctiveness of the specials was expected. After all, on duty they are viewed as police officers, something they themselves noted, rarely being identified as in any way different from the regular. The degree of responsibility and power incumbent on *every* special is considerable, hence the need for caution. In any event the specials have been keen to promote themselves as an efficient reserve modelled on the regulars, and ambitions to raise standards have paralleled initiatives to restrict recruitment to those meeting increasingly higher minimum standards (Police Advisory Board 1976, 1981). Thus, while physical requirements may be relaxed for specials, many forces now require specials to take the same initial recruitment test as regulars, although the pass mark *may* be relaxed slightly. In any event, the legal powers incumbent on specials make selection a crucial issue.

At the other extreme, we found examples of probation volunteers who were selected after an initial conversation with an officer. This was especially, but not exclusively the case, with those who were not accredited, but these could, none the less, be involved in a wide variety of tasks. Similarly, in one victim-support scheme volunteers were selected exclusively from another voluntary organization. For most volunteers in these two organizations, though, the rigorousness of the selection process lies somewhere between this extreme and the police norm. There was certainly more flexibility in probation and victim support because of local autonomy and the lack of formal guidelines (in terms of suitability).

So what are the implications of these findings? First, it is necessary to stress caution in talking about selection criteria for organizations *per se* since there are variations within them, especially where guidelines are non-existent or, as in the accreditation system, are not always followed. If agencies (like the specials) are keen that only people falling within a strict set of criteria should be recruited, the need for a formal system is evident. For probation and victim support this was deemed less necessary.

Second, it needs to be underlined that the type of selection procedure determines who gets selected. This is, of course, to state the obvious. We refer to it here only because the class bias of volunteers is frequently raised by agencies without recognition of their role in propagating it.

Third, rigorous selection procedures, and those not administered with sufficient diligence, can result in the process being a lengthy one. Many specials mentioned this, and the consequences for morale (even leading to loss of interest) should not be underestimated. Conversely, volunteers can be made to feel 'wanted' and gain pride from having successfully jumped the hurdles towards being accepted as a volunteer (a point covered in the next chapter).

Fourth, and this point is rarely acknowledged, agencies need to consider the consequences of rejecting a volunteer. If a person's offer of (free) help is refused it may have implications for his/her future community spirit. Clearly it should come as no surprise if a rejected volunteer feels resentful and offended. Certainly some personnel in each of the agencies recognized the need to channel 'unsuitable' people to other areas. That many did not is cause for concern. However, for those who are accepted, the key is to involve and integrate them into the organization. It is to this issue that we now turn.

The provision of work and a training programme are the essence of integrating volunteers. However, whereas research studies of policing have emphasized the value of training in inculcating the police culture (Banton 1973; Fielding 1988) within the volunteer literature the value of training has been debated largely in the context of providing information and skills necessary for the volunteer task (Aves 1969; Barr 1971). True, Aves in particular has covered the debate as to whether volunteers should be trained, thereby making them more akin to the professional and in turn threatening their voluntary status. Still, discussion about the role of training as a means of integrating volunteers and of outlining the 'ideology' and values of the organization has been overlooked.

Clearly training will be deemed more necessary for some tasks than for others. Certainly *all* specials and victim-support volunteers could be expected to impart specialist advice as part of their voluntary work. Probation volunteers are rather different though. Some working with clients, say with financial problems, would presumably benefit from knowledge about the DSS. Similarly, those in befriending or group work may require counselling skills. At the same time it is less obvious that involvement in running football teams, writing to prisoners, or transporting clients to court or prison necessitates specific training.[5]

Perhaps not surprisingly, therefore, both specials and victim-support-scheme volunteers were significantly more likely than probation volunteers to consider training as *necessary*. However, the suggestion that this merely reflects the facts that not all of the latter required specialist knowledge is to oversimplify the issue, and for a number of reasons.

First, probation volunteers' work is always the responsibility of the professional, and some probation officers made a point in meetings of stressing this fact. In victim support the co-ordinator assumes the role of adviser, but the volunteer is responsible for the case. Similarly, in the specials, we have noted that, although a regular officer would when present adopt the main role at an incident, specials sometimes had to make an arrest.

Second, it is likely that probation volunteers were less inclined to value training because many had not received any! For them training was not in practice an automatic requirement of becoming a volunteer. While the service recommended that they should receive training, it was not enshrined in agency regulations in quite the same way as for police and victim support. Certainly probation volunteers complained that programmes were disorganized, and this may in turn have led them to considering training as *unnecessary*. Similarly, if they had coped without any training, that too could be relevant in their doubting its necessity.

However, what of the value of training in inculcating the culture, and in integrating the volunteer? The specials were the only group to undertake regular and continuous training. For victim-support volunteers training was provided on their induction to the agency and then with occasional refreshers, often at volunteer meetings. This was also true for some – but not all – probation volunteers. The advantages for specials then are well illustrated. Specials, by being required to attend at the station regularly, were provided with an opportunity to meet other specials, organize duties and access and learn the police sub-culture. At the same time, on-going training was evidence to the specials that their work was recognized. In summary it facilitated involvement in the police.

THE VOLUNTEER PROCESS RECONSIDERED

At this point we must pause to take stock. We have considered the initial five stages of the volunteer process in terms of whether the decision is individual or agency based, and is sequential. The latter, at least, is problematic, and Figure 6.1 should not be interpreted too literally. To illustrate this and deviations from the model, we can cite four hypothetical examples of the processes involved:

- Volunteer A (Sheila): Sheila, a new student at the university, is interested in transferring to a social-work course and is told that she needs more relevant practical experience. She visits the local volunteer bureau where, after a long discussion, she is directed towards the probation service. Her application is accepted and she is invited to a volunteer meeting.
  Process: A B C D E; emphasis on volunteer bureau and career reasons.
- Volunteer B (Dawn): During a management-committee meeting of the victim-support scheme, the need for new volunteers is raised. Jim, the local vicar, mentions Dawn, a member of his congregation, whom he thinks might be interested. The committee feels that Dawn sounds an ideal prospect, and Jim is left to approach her. This he does. Dawn has not really thought about doing voluntary work but agrees that she has time on her hands and joins the new training programme.
  Process: D B A/C E; emphasis on word of mouth and drift.
- Volunteer C (Jackie): A local probation team decides it needs to recruit more volunteers and puts posters in local shop windows. Jackie, a newcomer to the area, who is feeling a bit lost, reads the advertisement when she goes in to buy her local paper and contacts the office. Following an informal interview and suitable references she is invited along to a volunteer meeting.
  Process: B A/C D E; emphasis on media recruitment and self-directed.

● Volunteer D (Anne): Anne has always been fascinated by the excitement of police work, but, with a secure and well-paid job in psychiatry, is not interested in a police career. Following a case conference at which the police were represented, she discusses the special constabulary with a WPC in the canteen and decides to apply to become a special. After a rigorous selection procedure, she is scheduled for an induction course.
Process: A/C B D E; emphasis on word-of-mouth recruitment and agency-led reasons.

These four imaginary cases illustrate just some of the various routes into voluntary work. Whatever the ordering of events, however, a series of decisions taken by individuals and agencies culminates in the acceptance of (some) applicants as volunteers.

Initial reasons for wanting to do voluntary work, the image presented by the agency, and the ways in which it is presented, decisions regarding agency choice, agency policies on selecting or rejecting applicants and agencies' policies vis-à-vis integration – together these culminate in specific individuals being recruited by a specific agency. We are at this stage led to reassess the outcome of these processes. Are those who become volunteers with an agency, represented by one of our three samples of current volunteers, distinctive from volunteers elsewhere, and if so in what aspects?

THE OUTCOME OF THE PROCESS: COMPARING VOLUNTEERS

We can compare these three groups of volunteers on two levels; first, in terms of their social characteristics (class, age, gender, etc.), second in terms of their perspectives with regard to a range of issues.

Taking gender first: volunteers in probation and victim support were alike in having a slight majority of female volunteers (56 per cent and 59 per cent respectively). Not surprisingly, police specials were, in contrast, predominantly male (79 per cent). The special constabulary, as part of a male-dominated organization and a masculine subculture (Holdaway 1983) inevitably appeals more to males. However, it is notable that for both police and probation, females were over-represented among volunteers compared with regular officers. On this criterion, then, females tended to be over-represented for all three volunteer groups.

This might have been expected, given earlier research. However, findings on age were rather more surprising. The relative youth of special constables was to a certain extent accentuated by the (national) imposition of an age bar. Be this as it may, as is clearly illustrated in Table 6.3, there were considerable age differences between our three samples, with victim-support-scheme volunteers in the South-west typified as old, compared both with the other volunteer groups and with earlier research.

TABLE 6.3 Age of volunteers

Age	Probation volunteers n = 58	Police specials n = 51	VSS volunteers n = 55	Total n = 164
	%	%	%	%
18–30	14	26	2	13
31–40	24	26	20	23
41–50	26	35	16	26
51–60	19	14	20	18
61 or over	17	0	42	20
Total	100	101	100	100

The combined influence of age and gender meant that special constables were markedly different in terms of employment status, with 92 per cent employed. At the other extreme only 47 per cent of victim-support-scheme volunteers were employed, with 21 per cent housewives and 31 per cent retired, illustrating the attraction to schemes of volunteers who would be available to make daytime visits. However, this scarcely explains the dearth of unemployed volunteers in our samples – none in victim support, one in the police and 13 per cent in probation – illustrating a tremendous untapped potential.

As a result of the distinctive employment status of volunteers, assessment of social class according to current occupation of volunteer or spouse was based on only a minority of victim-support-scheme volunteers. However, as is illustrated in Table 6.4 there were considerable and significant differences between the three groups, which were maintained when we included previous occupations of retired volunteers and when we used data from agency records on much larger samples. In general, victim-support-scheme volunteers were disproportionately drawn from social classes I and II, with almost none in semi- or unskilled manual work. Probation volunteers were, to a lesser extent, disproportionately middle class. In contrast, special constables included a slight majority in manual work, although even here most of these were in skilled occupations. A similar contrast emerged when we compared volunteer groups according to educational background. Special constables were significantly less likely to have secondary qualifications or a higher education than the other groups, with victim-support-scheme volunteers slightly ahead of probation.

How far then can these differences be explained by considering the type of agency concerned? As already noted, the police world is macho and therefore likely to attract male volunteers, and similarly the nature of police work at the grass roots may be more attractive to working-class people.

TABLE 6.4 Social class of volunteers

Social classes	Probation volunteers n = 32	Police specials n = 49	VSS volunteers n = 27	Total n = 108
	%	%	%	%
I and II	56	33	63	47
III non-manual	25	25	33	27
III manual, IV and V	19	43	4	26
Total	100	101	100	100

In contrast the need for victim-support volunteers to be available all day, but especially in the mornings, encourages reliance on housewives and the retired. It is perhaps surprising that the unemployed were excluded.[6] Probation volunteers were the most eclectic group. They were involved in a wide variety of tasks from writing letters to prisoners, and organizing groups, to transporting clients and their families, befriending offenders and assuming the role of a probation officer. Possibly because of this, they were therefore able to involve a wider variety of people.

Thus, although we might question the strict applicability of the traditional stereotype, we can at the same time explain differences in terms of the type of work or type of organization in question. Are there though different organizations for different people? To answer this question we need to go beyond a consideration of personal characteristics to assess the views, perspectives and indeed ideologies of those concerned. Can we assume that the type of person who wishes to become a special would not want to join the probation service as a volunteer, both because the ideology of the organization is different, and because so too is the work? After all, both these groups noted an interest in the organization as we indicated earlier. At the same time victim support provide an interesting mix, having evolved from both police and probation initiative. Their volunteers might thus be expected to share with the police an identification with the victim and with the probation service an interest in welfare-orientated work.

We thus incorporated within the study a variety of questions to test ideological perspectives. Initially we asked volunteers to state their agreement with certain types of 'hard' and 'soft' sentences for adult offenders. Later we asked a series of questions designed to ascertain their perspectives towards police, offenders and the crime problem using a revised version of an attitude scale used by Bottoms *et al.* (1987). They were all then asked two questions regarding political opinions.

If we first consider attitudes towards 'law and order' issues, one further question is of interest. Towards the end of the interview, we incorporated an additional question on motives for joining the agency, asking respondents to

TABLE 6.5 Comparison of mean-scale scores for three groups of volunteers

	Probation volunteers	VSS volunteers	Specials
Police scale	18.74	21.06	22.18
Crime-problem scale	16.84	18.55	19.1
Offender scale	16.25	20.32	20.65

rank a series of alternatives on a prompt card. In all nine alternatives were listed of which seven were identical for all three agencies. In retrospect, we decided to put less emphasis on the replies to this question compared with the open-ended alternatives, partly because it excluded the notion of 'drift', partly because respondents appeared drawn towards the more socially acceptable answers. Nevertheless two points can be made to illustrate the different perspectives of the three samples. First, victim-support-scheme volunteers ranked second the fact that 'Victims of crime were a group who particularly needed assistance', illustrating an identification with the victim.[7]

Second, the influence of being 'committed to the need to uphold law and order' was ranked fourth by *both* victim-support-scheme volunteers and special constables but only seventh by probation volunteers, suggesting a closer identification with 'law and order' perspectives among the first two groups of volunteers.

The pattern is reproduced when we consider scores on the three attitude scales, concerning police, offenders and the crime problem. On all three scales, as Table 6.5 illustrates, police specials and probation volunteers were distinct from one another, with the former more positive towards the police, more willing to distance themselves from offenders and more likely to consider that there was a serious crime problem in contemporary Britain.

Moreover, on all three scales the views of victim-support volunteers paralleled those of police specials. This is well illustrated if we consider the distribution of scale scores for the offender scale. As is evident from Figure 6.3, the scores for both police and victim-support volunteers were skewed towards the higher end of the scale (with the modal group 21–25), whilst for probation volunteers there was a skew towards the lower end.

However, a slightly different picture emerged when we compared attitudes towards a range of sentencing alternatives which might have been considered appropriate for some adult offenders (Mawby and Gill 1987: 213). Again specials reflected a more punitive philosophy: they were most likely to favour capital and corporal punishment and least likely to see probation or community service orders as appropriate. In general, however, victim-support volunteers were far closer to those of probation volunteers and only differed to the extent that both

FIGURE 6.3   Comparison of offender-scale scores for the three groups of volunteers

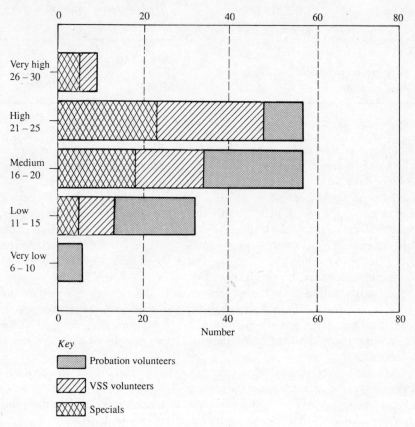

Key

Probation volunteers

VSS volunteers

Specials

they and police specials were rather less likely than probation volunteers to see the caution as ever appropriate for adults.

Overall then it appears that victim-support volunteers shared with specials a definition of the crime problem but preferred probation volunteers' solutions. Certainly, in broad terms at least, the ideology of the volunteers appears similar to that of the organization and there is support for notions of a subculture for volunteers within an organization.

If we were to translate these ideas on to a political level, we might expect the specials to vote Conservative to a greater extent than the other two groups of volunteers. Similarly we may expect probation volunteers to identify least with the right-wing view. To test out this hypothesis we asked our respondents who they had voted for in the previous general election (May 1983) and who they would vote for if there was an election the following day.

Looking first at the figures for previous voting behaviour, it was clear that specials most strongly identify with the Conservative party, and only amongst probation volunteers was there any notable support for Labour, although even here the Conservatives were still the most popular party. Victim-support volunteers were again somewhere in between: the Conservative vote was the most popular and there was a strong tendency not to vote Labour.

Future voting intentions reflected the traditional swing away from the party in government and the fact that this was a period of Alliance growth, especially in the South-west. However, the specials were still the most likely to vote Tory and probation volunteers least likely. Furthermore, only amongst probation volunteers was there any notable support for Labour which had remained fairly steady against an across-the-board swing to the Alliance.[8] Victim-support volunteers could again be seen as having views somewhere between the other two groups.

STAYING INVOLVED

The final stage of the process outlined in Figure 6.2 concerns continued involvement with the agency. We can thus at this stage ask how the various decisions taken by individual and agency which result in individuals starting voluntary work in one of the three agencies further affect their willingness (or otherwise) to remain with the agency.

Volunteers' commitment towards voluntary work may in part be judged by their extent of involvement in it. This though carries a problematic assumption: that everyone has the same opportunity, in terms of both personal time available, and supply of work from the organization. Clearly this is not the case and our organizations highlight this. Victim-support schemes were relatively new, and with a lack of referrals some volunteers had not been offered an opportunity of contacting a victim. Against this though, of those who had visited a victim, most were happy to revisit and few placed restrictions on who they would or would not feel able to help.

Lack of work was particularly a problem for probation volunteers. Indeed, 41 per cent were inactive at the time of the interview, compared with only 6 per cent of specials. Moreover, of those engaged in voluntary work more specials committed more hours weekly than either of the other groups of volunteers. Again though the nature of the work was different, and this will explain in some way the differences here.

The amount of time a volunteer has spent with an agency may well tell us something about commitment, although this is less relevant for victim support, given its recent origins. Nevertheless, when probation and police are compared, some interesting results appear. Whereas a third of specials had served for over twelve years, the same was true for only two probation volunteers. Similarly, while over a half of the latter had served for less than three years, the same was true for only a quarter of specials. Of course, periods of service cannot be isolated from reasons for joining, and it will be recalled that between a quarter and a fifth had cited career ambitions for becoming a probation volunteer. In this context it may have been expected that their length of service would be shorter, and unrelated to commitment, since having gained the experience they would presumably wish to move on to pursue their career ambitions. This is evident from replies to the questionnaires given to resigning volunteers. Against this though, specials did most frequently state a specific interest in the organization. Commitment then is clearly bound up with motivations and organizational policy and structure. It would be on very tentative grounds to suggest on the evidence presented that the specials were the most committed, although the pointers are in that direction. What we can go on to show is that organizational arrangements made it easier for specials to feel favourably disposed towards their voluntary work.

The provision of work and ongoing training encouraged more advantages for specials. It enabled them to meet people. Indeed specials were significantly more likely than the other two groups to say they had friends who were volunteers in their own agency. In addition, specials were significantly more likely than probation volunteers to spend their leisure time with either other volunteers or professionals in their own agency and also have friends who were professionals within their agency.

The training sessions themselves were more sociable for specials. They took place in the police station, which contains the police bar, and the opportunity to socialize afterwards was therefore ever present and commonly accepted. Meetings of probation volunteers usually took place in the probation offices (which had no bar), although sometimes someone's house was preferred. Normally a cup of coffee during the meeting and informal chat afterwards was the limit of interaction. Victim-support meetings were sometimes held in the police station, and the availability of the bar encouraged some to socialize, but this was less customary than for specials. In any event, where meetings were held elsewhere, little attempt was made to maintain contact after the formal business of the meeting was concluded.

Volunteers' views though can perhaps best be understood in terms of why they continue with their voluntary work. During our study we asked them precisely this question. Table 6.6 displays the results.

Of particular interest is the relative degree of emphasis on 'enjoyment'. It is usually assumed that a person's reasons for continuance in voluntary work are related to levels of satisfaction. In the case of specials our findings bear this out. Indeed, given the information presented in this chapter so far, the specials' emphasis here is predictable. They were, after all, the most integrated into the agency. Another expected finding here is the greater proportion of victim-support volunteers who claimed to be 'agency-committed' or continued for reasons of 'stickability'. Schemes were new and struggling to establish an identity. Many volunteers had undertaken few, if any, cases. It would have been surprising had a lot claimed they enjoyed their work. Rather they were part of an organization establishing itself against, from many police officers among others,

TABLE 6.6 Primary reason for continuing with voluntary work

	Probation volunteers n = 58	Police specials n = 51	VSS volunteers n = 55	Total n = 164
	%	%	%	%
Enjoyment	38	63	15	38
Other-directed	28	2	27	20
Self-directed	9	16	2	9
Agency-committed	5	10	24	13
Stickability	3	2	15	7
Religious	0	0	6	2
Career	2	0	0	1
Not active	16	8	13	12
Total	101	101	102	102

scepticism (at least judged by the low number of referrals). They were committed to their schemes (agency-committed) and some believed that once such a commitment was initiated it should be seen through to its conclusion (stickability).

At least one other important difference between samples requires emphasis: that is the relative emphasis on the other-directed and self-directed categories; in particular the distinctiveness of specials compared with probation and victim-support volunteers. Notwithstanding a difference between these latter two groups on the self-directed category, the findings lend support to a dichotomy between caring and non-caring work. Other-directed reasons were most important for victim-support volunteers, and second in importance for probation volunteers, but only one special identified this reason for continued involvement.

Moreover, and by contrast, 'self-directed' was the second most popular category for specials, but only one victim-support volunteer mentioned such a motive. So while reasons for continuance seem different from reasons for joining, we can also add that emphases on helping other people or benefiting oneself are more identifiable along organizational lines in terms of caring and non-caring work than they are in the context of motivations for voluntary work. But at this point, of course, volunteers may have been inculcated with the ideology of the agency.

What does emerge therefore is the relevance of organizational policy in terms of its ability to integrate; at the same time the type of organization structure is relevant too, and the opportunities it provides for active involvement of volunteers.

DISCUSSION

This chapter has sought to evaluate comparatively the motivations of volunteers, and their (lack of) integration and (lack of) role within the probation and police services and victim support. In so doing it has realized some interesting findings. It appears that in the early part of the volunteer process there are remarkable similarities between the three groups of volunteers; however, as volunteers become more influenced by the organization, more distinct differences begin to emerge, and these differences can, at least in part, be explained by the work, policy and ideology of the organization in question.

We looked first at the decision to volunteer, and it was revealed that, if career motivation was seen as a specific form of self-directed motivation, the similarity between the samples was striking. Indeed, our findings confirm those of Sherrott (1983) in that volunteers are primarily attracted to voluntary work by personal benefits. At the same time though the traditional way of describing volunteer motivations in terms of either egoism or altruism must be questioned in the light of other findings here. The organization is a crucial factor for some, religious beliefs for others, but of particular significance was the sizeable minority who drift. Indeed the drift effect was emphasized about as frequently as the much discussed philanthropic motive which we have termed 'other-directed'.

There was also a degree of similarity in reasons for joining a *particular* agency: an interest in the organization, career ambitions and drift predominated. We have noted that career intentions were cited mostly by probation volunteers, especially in relation to future employment with the probation service. We therefore saw scope for suggesting that this could be described as a type of interest in the organization. For specials, though, interest in the organization was quite emphatic and no doubt a reflection of the distinctive nature of police work. Conversely victim support is of more recent origin and, while this very point will have attracted some, many were largely unaware of victim support until they were invited to join.

The drift effect, which has been overlooked by past researchers as a reason for joining, nevertheless complements the findings of ourselves with others that recruitment frequently revolves around a word-of-mouth strategy. If people volunteer because they are asked to join a particular agency, clearly they may be seen as drifting into a particular type of voluntary work. Of course, those who are asked or approached about undertaking voluntary work or have an interest in the organization are likely to be acceptable volunteers. If they are not, then agency selection procedures ensure these people are weeded out. This is important because it means only certain people are left, 'the right people'. This is crucial to the development of distinctive groups of volunteers, even more so in other agencies at the high-status end of the continuum we presented in Figure 2.2.

However, faced with a person willing to be a volunteer, how does each agency decide who is suitable? Looking at personal characteristics it was possible to discern inter-organizational differences. Probation and victim-support volunteers were similar but the latter contained higher proportions of elderly and housewives because, we suggested, the nature of the work required that they be available at short notice and particularly during the day. Both groups contained a majority of women and middle-class volunteers. The specials were different again, but the larger working-class and male element reflects the perceived nature of police work (and the police service is male dominated anyway), making it more likely to attract this type of person. Probation volunteers formed the most eclectic group, possibly because the work they could do was more varied.

Just as other writers have used the notion of ideologies to differentiate between workers (Hardiker 1977; Smith and Harris 1982), so too we considered ideologies as a basis for comparison. Here we found that there were ideological variations between the samples and that these were in accord with those of the agency. Thus probation volunteers favoured softer sentences, had a less rosy picture of the police, saw offenders in a more favourable light, were less concerned about the crime problem and identified more closely with the middle ground of British politics, while specials were the antithesis of this, with victim support somewhere between the two. Indeed victim-support volunteers seemed to share with the police a similar perspective on the crime problem, offenders and the police, but favoured probation-service solutions (treatment in preference to punishment).

There was then, within each agency, a distinct group of people; and this is a basis upon which volunteer subcultures might be formed. However, we need to guard against over-simplifying the issue. After all there were intra-organization differences. It is, for example, perhaps surprising that, if the organization has an ideological appeal, four in ten probation volunteers favoured capital and corporal punishment. There did appear to be less variation in the specials. How can this be explained? At this point we need to reconsider the way in which volunteers are integrated, that is through training programmes and the provision of work.

We have argued that training is not only important in enhancing skills and knowledge; it also facilitates communication of the organization's values. Here police-training policies were salient. The ongoing training programme was a constant reminder of police views. At the same time it afforded the opportunity to meet and build up a rapport with other regulars and specials. This was enhanced by the presence of the police bar which encouraged socialization and thereby access to the police subculture. Specials were thus able to identify with the regular police and their values, and regular contacts provided the opportunity for this common set of values to be translated into group identification and solidarity (for a further discussion see Gill and Mawby 1990).

For victim support an initial training programme was available, supplemented by ongoing meetings, and, while these often took place in the police station, they were less frequent and were not to the same extent in their own territory as was the case for specials. In contrast, the latter were able to establish an identity with the police station; it was 'their' station. Perhaps because of this there was far less of a tendency for victim-support volunteers to socialize in this way after a meeting. It thus seemed that, while group members shared similar backgrounds and views, lack of contact meant that the development of a victim-support subculture was restricted to identification with a cause, rather than a group of peers.

Probation volunteers fared worse. Many had received no training at all, and many of those who had commented on its disorganization. This limited the extent to which the service was able to inculcate its values and integrate the volunteer. Thus, while volunteers were extremely positive about the probation service and reflected many of its official objectives, the opportunity for this to develop into a shared group solidarity was lost.

But what about the provision of work? Again for specials there were distinct advantages: the opportunities for voluntary work were far greater. Policing is a 24-hour activity; that specials could work alone, or with other specials, or with other regulars increased their opportunities for involvement. Moreover because they could, and most did at some point work with a regular, it provided them with a model, it increased the number of people they knew and thereby enhanced integration. Furthermore they wore a uniform and this provided a sense of identity with the police service; they were recognized as police officers by the general public. Again probation and victim-support volunteers were less fortunate in that they suffered from a lack of work, obviously limiting the extent to which they could become involved. Apart from this the professional, especially in the case of victim support, was somewhat distanced from the volunteer.

The role of the organization then is clearly vital; where volunteers are able to build up a rapport with each other, meet on a regular basis and become directly involved in the work, commitment will be stronger and a volunteer subculture may emerge. That more probation volunteers appeared to be at tangents with the ideology of the organization is at least partly because the probation service was less efficient in inculcating its beliefs and values. Were the service to do so by providing regular training and meetings and regular work for all volunteers, we would expect the situation to change. It is to this issue of organizing volunteers that we now turn.

7

ORGANIZING VOLUNTEERS

INTRODUCTION

Most studies of the voluntary sector have indicated a variety of organizational types in existence (Brenton 1985; Hatch 1980; Wolfenden 1978). So, too, in this project, following Hatch (1982), we have identified different types of volunteers. Given these variations, the difficulties of presenting a uniform policy as to the best ways of organizing volunteers are evident. Not surprisingly, perhaps, those policy documents which do exist tend to remain in-house, and refer to one agency, although recently the British Association of Social Workers (BASW) has produced a publication on organizing volunteers in the social services which would be of more general relevance (Ridley and Currie 1987), and the Volunteer Centre produce some useful information sheets.[1] Here though we wish to focus on the three agencies studied, assessing the way the organization and policies affect volunteers and their role. Our aim is to identify some issues relevant to the best ways of using volunteers as derived from our comparative study. We do not propose to offer a comprehensive information package on organizing volunteers. Our data are not of that order. Rather we wish to explain and identify issues which have evolved in our study, which may guide those interested in the area of organizing volunteers.

The first part of this chapter will consider the role of the professional and the type of organization as it relates to organizing volunteers; from here more specific policy objectives will be discussed, considering recruiting and selecting, training, co-ordinating and deploying volunteers. The final part will discuss the problem of over-identification which has previously received little attention in the volunteer literature.

THE PROFESSIONAL AND THE ORGANIZATION

We have already noted that partnerships between professionals and volunteers exist in both the voluntary and statutory fields. However, during the time of our research, the voluntary organization, that is victim support, contained volunteers only. In essence this afforded a more detailed appraisal of the role of the professional as it relates to volunteer use. Professionals, both police and probation officers, acted as gatekeepers to involvement in voluntary work and at the same time served as role models. That this dual role existed for probation volunteers and specials but not, in the latter respect, for victim-support volunteers is important. Probation and police volunteers needed as *individuals* to prove their worthiness of involvement in the work of the organization. In the case of victim support, proof of one's value to the gatekeepers, the police, was incumbent upon the *organization*, or more specifically, the committee rather than the individual, and a crucial distinction. First, though, let us consider the case of probation volunteers and specials.

There are a number of good reasons to suppose that police officers more than probation officers would resist the use of volunteers. Traditionally the police have been sceptical of outsiders (Holdaway 1983) and, since rule breaking is endemic (D. Smith 1986), specials clearly pose a direct threat. There is considerably more evidence of rule breaking amongst police than probation officers, although this may be due in part to the lack of research of the latter. Moreover, it remains true that police volunteers are far more likely than their probation counterparts to work alongside the professional, doing the same tasks at the same times, thereby enabling police work to be more visible to these 'outsiders'.

Certainly our research findings, reported earlier, reveal a more apparent undercurrent of discontent amongst police than is the case for probation officers. However, as we illustrated in the previous chapter, it was very much the specials who appeared the most integrated. They were certainly the more active and were most likely to say they continued in their voluntary work for reasons for enjoyment. How then can this apparent contradiction be explained?

For a moment we need to move away from a specific focus on policy to a consideration of the nature of the work of the agency. For specials there was a greater availability of work. Policing is a 24-hour activity, and since specials could either accompany regulars or specials or patrol alone the potential of involvement was considerable. Moreover, whereas most specials were involved in 'real police work' (certainly potentially), many probation volunteers were on the margins of probation practice. Certainly probation volunteers were less likely to work alongside and with the professionals and this limited their integration; specials had greater contact and consequently they were able to identify more readily with the organization and attempt to prove their value to more sceptical officers.

This process was further encouraged, and made easier for the specials, by the importance accredited to the bar: nearly all police stations contain bars. This enabled specials to meet each other and regulars in an informal atmosphere; friendships developed and this made the experience of being a volunteer all the more enjoyable. At the same time specials could be identified as part of the police: it was 'their' police station, they were privileged members of the police social club. Finally, specials wear uniforms, and this further enhanced their identity with the police service.

Such provision was not available for probation volunteers. There are no bars in probation offices and there is less of a tradition of meeting socially. Furthermore, probation volunteers do not wear uniforms and as such could not be identified as volunteers, nor perhaps build up an identity with the probation service quite so easily. In all then, they appeared less integrated.

There is a further point which should be stressed here. We have placed considerable emphasis on the police subculture and the extent to which this breeds suspicion of outsiders. Although this was initially a barrier to volunteers, once specials had overcome this barrier, their own senses of identity as police officers was reinforced. Indeed it will be recalled that specials considered officers to have a more positive attitude to them personally than they did towards the special constabulary as a whole. They recognized their own position as one of privilege; scepticism from officers was recognized but seen as directed against *other* specials. So, while for probation volunteers there was not an obvious subcultural barrier to integration, there were equally none of the advantages which can be derived from a shared identity with a group of people.

For victim-support volunteers, two issues are particularly salient. One concerns the separate identity of the referrer. The other focuses on the relative recency of victim-support development.

Victim-support volunteers have very little contact with the police[2] who are, of course, the main referrers. It was difficult for them to prove their value and *bona fides* and therefore increase their acceptability and the value of the organization to the police, and thereby increase the number of referrals. So even if an individual volunteer had assisted a victim with a complex problem, there was no guarantee, indeed, there was very little chance of either the police referrer, or the officer who initially attended the scene of the crime, ever being made aware of this. True, all committees contained police representatives who, it was hoped, would hear about volunteers' work and convey this message to other officers. However, in practice it was impossible for all officers to be made aware of the good work of each volunteer. In all then, there was a lack of work for volunteers which limited their integration; at the same time remedies were the responsibility not of themselves but of another body, the committee.

An additional but related issue is that victim-support schemes were new. Initially this was sufficient to maintain volunteers' interest – indeed it will be recalled that agency commitment and 'stickability' featured prominently in volunteers' stated reasons for continuing with their voluntary work – although clearly this is likely to have limits. Certainly one scheme folded because of, in part, a lack of referrals, and at least one co-ordinator was so disillusioned over this issue to consider resignation and was only prevented by having been cajoled by the vice-chairman. Moreover, when victim-support volunteers were asked how the scheme could be improved, the most frequent answer was the need for more referrals! Victim-support schemes then suffered from being voluntary organizations detached from the hand that provided the work, and also from being new and without an established identity. Additionally, volunteers did not appear to socialize together regularly. Nor, of course, did they have a uniform to aid their identification.

In all, the following situation was apparent. The specials were well integrated into the police:[3] they worked alongside and did the same types of tasks as regular officers; they could socialize at the police station; and, although subcultural barriers were apparent, once overcome integration was demonstrated. Organizational factors facilitated specials' involvement. For probation volunteers contact with probation officers was frequently confined to advice when required and when sought by the volunteer. Because other contact was minimal, it was frequently difficult to convince autonomy-minded officers of volunteers' keenness to make them aware of their availability. For victim-support volunteers contact with the professional was even further removed and they too suffered from a lack of work, although, because schemes were new, many volunteers were committed to part of what was considered an innovative and worthwhile cause.

At this juncture though we need to move away from a consideration of organizational factors to a focus on policy. More specifically we need to discuss those areas where at least one of our agencies did or could implement a policy to improve the integration and performance of volunteers. First, we shall look at recruitment and selection.

RECRUITING AND SELECTION OF VOLUNTEERS

Even in the early years of the welfare state Beveridge and Wells (1949) were writing of the need for a voluntary sector; participation for all was seen as an essential ingredient for democracy. Nevertheless as we have shown, a sequence of studies has questioned the extent to which all types of people participate. Certainly more recently some working-class groups of volunteers have evolved (particularly *vis-à-vis* self-help groups), but in most areas of the welfare state a bias in terms of middle-age, middle-class, female, married volunteers has been repeated. Notwithstanding our own observations of the generalization involved in this stereotype, what has been rather less commented upon is the extent to which an agency's policy has contributed to this bias. In other words, the almost widespread comment about the typical volunteer has not included discussions about the role of agency policies in perpetuating those biases.

To suggest that only certain types of people offer services as volunteers is only a partial explanation, and anyway a simplification. The drift effect we have identified is an indication that people can be persuaded to volunteer. In any event we found evidence of quite strict selection procedures. Most probation volunteers and victim-support volunteers submitted an application and underwent an interview, and for specials there is in addition, an examination. While we do appreciate the need for screening – not least for ensuring that volunteers are acquainted with agency expectations of them – we do wish to add a caveat.

It strikes us as important that a discussion about who becomes a volunteer should not be divorced from the part played by agency policies in determining that selection. At present organizations pay only lip service to the benefits of volunteers in democratizing the system and affording local accountability. These issues need to be considered in volunteer use.

There needs to be an appreciation of who is required and for what purposes, and guidelines given to ensure that selectors are aware of the benefits of representativeness amongst volunteers. At present we have little confidence that professionals are aware of the value of volunteers in this respect. In our survey of probation officers and police officers such comments were absent when asked about the benefits of volunteers in their own agency.

Part of the problem is the low priority professional training courses accord to volunteer-related issues. It is certainly a neglected aspect of social work courses (Gill and Andrews 1987). During our research the same point was made by police officers about police training. The need for professionals to be trained in use of volunteers is not a new one: far from it. That we should have to emphasize it again here is symptomatic of the traditional neglect of volunteers by organizations, and yet it is crucial to the effectiveness of all other policies.

Overall, we found a wealth of support for a policy of deploying volunteers locally; few volunteers in any of the agencies cited difficulties, most commented on the advantages. Perhaps more emphasis could be placed on recruiting volunteers through advertisements in shop windows and libraries.[4] These would advertise the work locally and add meaning to local accountability. It does appear that the volunteer potential is not being thwarted by volunteers, but rather by professionals and the agencies that employ them.

TRAINING VOLUNTEERS

In the volunteer literature a range of studies has discussed the value of training in providing volunteers with the knowledge and skills to pursue their activity confidently (Aves 1969; Barr 1971; Ridley and Currie 1987). It was a point emphasized by the vast majority of our sample. This was particularly the case for specials and victim-support volunteers, all of whom had undergone or were undergoing training. Of course, for specials this is always ongoing, and most victim-support schemes supplemented their initial package with monthly meetings which incorporate training at least periodically. That probation volunteers commonly lacked training programmes and ongoing meetings was a frequent cause of lament (although a few, who had no or little experience of any training, questioned that they were necessary at all). Training may therefore operate as a reflection of agency interest in the volunteer. Certainly this, allied to the potential for inculcating the values of the organization and in building up a rapport amongst volunteers, leads us to conclude that arguments against the training of volunteers – for example, that it makes them more like the professional, hence losing the quality of being distinctly different (Aves 1969) – were insufficient to outweigh the advantages of properly organized programmes.

However, we are able to make a number of comments about the way training was organized. In particular we would argue the benefits of a joint training programme, something that has received remarkably little attention in the volunteer literature. Certainly with regard to our three groups there was plenty of overlap in the training packages or, perhaps more importantly, there was sufficient scope and benefit in a core programme for all three groups. There would be a number of advantages.

First, it would result in a more informed understanding of the criminal-justice system, since each could learn about each other's work. Hence it would serve as a public-relations device. Second, it would encourage inter-agency co-operation. Third, it would involve a pooling of resources which ultimately may benefit the hard-pressed voluntary sector. Fourth, given that many people appear to drift into voluntary work, it is possible that some are not engaged in the activity most closely allied to their interests or needs. A joint training package preceding their entrance into an agency would facilitate a more informed decision. It would also enable volunteers to understand issues relevant to the volunteer role. At present volunteers appear at least as ignorant as professionals of concepts such as 'accountability', 'participation' and 'democracy' as they relate to volunteering. This may be particularly important for specials who, as we discuss later, tend to over-identify with the police.

The involvement of professionals in training is also crucial. This is standard in the police, although even here there is scope for involving more officers. In probation the norm was for the probation officer who was responsible for co-ordinating volunteers to undertake the training package and organize meetings. Some groups did involve other probation officers periodically or encouraged all others to attend occasionally; and in one group it was arranged for all officers to attend meetings/training sessions on a rotational basis. However, flexibility left open the possibility that training was nonexistent or minimal, with little involvement from officers. In victim support also there was ample scope to invite more probation and particularly police officers to meetings and training sessions so that they could familiarize themselves with the others' role. One co-ordinator visited all shifts as they came on duty to explain the role of victim support with apparently beneficial results.

The involvement of professionals with volunteers is thus essential for both groups, and training sessions provide a recognizable way of facilitating this. At present it is a means which is needlessly under-utilized. Moreover, it is important for training to be sensitive to volunteers' comments and views. At this point the role of the co-ordinator becomes crucial.

CO-ORDINATING VOLUNTEERS

Effective supervision and co-ordination are essential to maximizing the potential volunteer (Quinne and Bazalgette 1979). Volunteer co-ordinators must be committed to their task. Additionally, two other conditions are necessary. The first is time to devote to their responsibilities; the second, status within the organization. To illustrate these points further, we can distinguish between local co-ordinators and regional or area co-ordinators.

Let us look first at local co-ordinators. In the probation service, where volunteers were usually – although not exclusively – organized around teams, a probation officer (sometimes the senior) was responsible for organizing volunteers. It was usual for a volunteer to be appointed chairperson to assist in the co-ordination of the volunteer group. For the most part though the two worked separately. The problem here centred on the probation officer having insufficient time to devote to his volunteer-related duties. Indeed, the officer had the status but not the time, while the volunteer chairperson frequently had the time but not the status necessary for the task.

In the police, the divisional training sergeant was responsible for co-ordinating specials with assistance from the specials' divisional commandant and sub-divisional officers. The respective role of the training sergeant and specials here tended to vary between divisions and was dependent to an extent on the personalities of the people concerned. Nevertheless there was still the problem, particularly with keen and enthusiastic divisional commandants, that they had the time but lacked the status within the police service, and as such were dependent on the training sergeants. Most of the time though the training sergeant who had the status lacked the time to devote to the specials, a concern which was frequently voiced.

Perhaps the most effective co-ordinators were those in victim-support schemes. They were all voluntary and frequently housewives or retired. They had both time and status within the organization.[5] Unfortunately though they lacked referrals and, although the co-ordinator could act on behalf of victim support, he or she clearly had no status within the police and hence lacked influence on a key policy issue. However, this is a somewhat different issue and in the context of victim support, co-ordinators appeared very effective.

Before we comment on this further, it is perhaps worth noting the regional structure for each agency. In the probation service there was very little formal organization, but in one area there were plans to arrange for the co-ordination of teams. In one sub-area a co-ordinator was employed for a while on a half-time basis. Unfortunately the individual delegated was not a probation officer and thus lacked status within the organization, and this in part thwarted some ambitious co-ordinating projects. In the police most of the regional co-ordination of specials was delegated to the force commandant. He is a former senior police officer, obviously familiar with police organizational practices, who is now retired and had time to commit to the specials. He had an office at headquarters which afforded him access to senior officers where he was ideally placed to co-ordinate specials' activities. Indeed, he was the resident 'expert' and regulars of all ranks contacted him for advice. The force commandant was indeed a very effective co-ordinator. In victim support the regional co-ordinator was a volunteer who acted as adviser and liaison with headquarters in London. Ironically she as a housewife had time but, because of the autonomy of local schemes, lacked status. Nevertheless she was a keen and able adviser.

So what lessons can we learn about organizing volunteers? First, with regard to probation and police services, it appears beneficial to have both a professional and volunteer responsible for co-ordinating volunteers both locally and regionally, with the lay person assisting the professional and acting as a volunteer voice. However, it is essential that professionals should be apportioned appropriate time and encouraged to fill that time co-ordinating volunteers. Job descriptions would clearly be helpful in assisting with that objective. Full-time and professional co-ordinators would be a major step in illustrating the priority of volunteers within an agency, and the value of harnessing the wealth of support within the community. If this appears naïve in the light of the pressure on resources, then attention need only be drawn to the potential benefits of properly co-ordinated volunteers; not least in terms of increasing resources!

Professionals as volunteer co-ordinators would at the same time give volunteers status within the organization. But volunteer co-ordinators are more likely to have status in the eyes of professionals if they are keen and knowledgeable. Here we wish to draw attention to the benefits of retired professionals returning to their organization to assist with volunteers. It appears to us to be an untapped source, yet in the police service we studied it worked effectively. Similarly, Hadley and Scott (1980) have noted the enormous untapped volunteer potential amongst the elderly.

Of course victim-support schemes, as noted in Chapter 5, are in a stage of transition; moving towards regional structures and paid co-ordinators as a result of central-government funding. Notwithstanding the general applause such initiatives have received, our text is perhaps a timely reminder of the crucial role of co-ordinators and the constant need to ensure that co-ordinating volunteers does not become secondary to their administrative duties.

There is one further point we would wish to make about the role of co-ordinators: that is the need to ensure they are properly prepared for their task. Richards (1977) is but one who has noted that organizing volunteers is a highly skilled task requiring expertise and specific training. Few of the co-ordinators in any of the agencies we studied had received any specific training for their task. This issue needs to be recognized and then rectified. One aspect of management relates to the effective deployment of volunteers, to which we now turn.

DEPLOYING VOLUNTEERS

Perhaps that most essential issue in terms of integrating volunteers is the provision of work. Since volunteers forsake financial rewards, they require alternative forms of recompense, and the provision of work is a minimum requirement. True it is possible to contend that some people volunteer for other reasons, such as status, and therefore will not automatically want to engage in work, their ambitions having been fulfilled by virtue of having become a volunteer. However, there was little evidence of this, and rigorous selection procedures should guard against it. Given this, providing volunteers with work and hence with involvement becomes essential.

What is probably most surprising therefore is that of all the complaints we received from volunteers during the course of the study, the most frequent was that they were under-utilized. Some probation and victim-support volunteers complained they had *never* been approached to take on a client. Probation volunteers were particularly frustrated at this since officers appeared to them to be so busy and yet they consistently overlooked one readily available means of reducing that burden. In victim support the issue was slightly different, since volunteers were aware of the efforts of the organization to rectify the referral deficiency. In any event, they were part of a new cause. Even specials, who were rarely without work altogether, were keen to become further involved.

Of course, it is not always possible to predict how many volunteers will be needed, particularly, for example, in a new victim-support scheme. One large rural scheme covering a whole police division had to recruit sufficient volunteers to cover the whole area. However, because of a poor referral policy and the difficulty of holding volunteer meetings because of the distances involved, inactivity was high. Elsewhere we have discussed the benefits of a direct or automatic referral policy rather than an indirect one (Mawby and Gill 1987). Here we draw attention to the benefits of organizing volunteers in small groups.

It is tempting to suggest that volunteers should only be recruited when there is an unequivocal need for them. This, however, is simplistic and even naïve given the information presented above. Nevertheless, volunteers were frequently recruited when there was very little chance that they could be usefully deployed. This runs counter to the emphasis of the training programme which builds up an eagerness among volunteers to become involved. Where therefore the availability of voluntary work is unpredictable, it seems good practice to advise volunteers of this on their induction to the agency. Indeed all volunteers should be advised of the expectations of them, and of ways of bringing attention to any grievances they have. Clearly, training, meetings and supervision are all relevant here, and each is a central part of integrating volunteers into the agency; the provision of work though is the key to volunteer morale.

Earlier we noted other ways of integrating volunteers, principally through socialization, and we focused on the advantages to the police in having a bar and social club of which specials were members. A rather different strategy was used by one senior probation officer who attempted to overcome some of the limits in the way the probation service integrated volunteers into the team. He ensured that all probation volunteers were aware that they were welcome to use office facilities. This included the staff common room, secretaries and telephones. The volunteers were given a notice board where messages could easily be left, hoping that it would be regularly used by volunteers and officers alike. While this initiative came at the end of the research period and thus was not open to evaluation, it was perhaps the most positive attempt at integrating volunteers within probation that we saw.

In a rather different way volunteers were sometimes invited to meetings of professionals. It was evidence to volunteers that they were recognized and was extremely popular, although rare. Sometimes volunteers were invited to conferences or exercises mainly designed for professionals and this again aided integration. In probation there were also a variety of imaginative, if sometimes complex, administrative schemes to ensure that all officers were aware of each volunteer's interests and availability. The point we wish to stress here is that there exists a variety of ways of integrating volunteers and hence adding to the resources of the agency. Moreover, as we hope we have illustrated, it requires far more than willing helpers; it necessitates a professional and considered approach backed by organizational will. At present too many agencies lack this commitment.

VOLUNTEERING FOR WHAT?

Underpinning issues of recruitment and selection, training, co-ordination and deployment there is one central question: for what work is one volunteering? In Chapter 2 we introduced the notion that in terms of agency appeal different organizations within the criminal justice system might attract different volunteers, with distinctive views of who 'deserved' their help, what benefits they could derive from their involvement, etc. At the same time, we put forward a classification of volunteers which, in terms of role, intra-agency specialism and commitment, implied that the tasks demanded by the agency of its volunteers could be quite different, both between and within agencies.

What then are the implications of these distinctions for ways of organizing volunteers? If we consider first the appeal of different organizations, there is clearly the danger of a circular process whereby agencies recruit volunteers who reconfirm the means and goals of the agency. For example, if a primary attraction of the special constabulary is the excitement and action which it promises, then volunteers prioritizing such goals will be recruited and attempts to shift the emphasis, for example towards more service-oriented or mundane tasks, like neighbourhood watch, will be frustrated. If some victim-support schemes prioritize victim needs with the implication that offenders receive undue consideration within the criminal justice system, those volunteers who are recruited cannot be expected to enthuse about involvement in mediation initiatives.

This leads us on to the somewhat broader issue of the volunteers' tasks. We have suggested that agencies traditionally have tended to recruit volunteers and then ask themselves what work the volunteers could do. This results in confusion, ambiguity and under-use of volunteers. However, within probation, police and victim support there is some indication of a shift towards, as one respondent put it, recruiting 'horses for courses'.

This has parallels with the rediscovery within social work of the generic team concept. Agencies may wish to deploy volunteers on a wide range of tasks and could be clearer at the recruitment stage as to what those tasks are. This would then affect recruitment, selection, and training. It has implications for the appeal of voluntary work to different potential volunteers, the suitability of volunteers to different tasks, and the practical viability of volunteers' carrying out certain tasks. For example, the opportunity to specialize in work with neighbourhood watch might attract a different type of applicant from that drawn to the special constabulary; mediation work might broaden the appeal of victim support; work with prisoners' wives might attract different volunteers to probation. Equally, some volunteers may be more suitable for administrative or legal-advice work rather than close involvement with individual clients.

The nature of the typical work carried out by volunteers may make volunteering impractical to a group of potential volunteers who could none the less carry out specific tasks. For example, it can be argued that in the rural South-west victim-support-scheme volunteers need a car and a telephone and should be available to assist a victim at short notice; in consequence, those in full-time employment, or without a car or telephone, will rarely be recruited and infrequently used. However, if victim-support schemes take on a responsibility for regular court work (Ralphs 1988), such tasks may be *feasible* to a different 'market' of potential recruits and indeed may *appeal* to different people.

This re-emphasizes the point made earlier in this chapter concerning interaction between volunteers deployed by different agencies. If, for example, a probation-service recruit volunteers to operate in the courtroom setting with defendants, and victim support does likewise for victims, it makes little sense to keep the two sets of volunteers apart until they coincidentally cross paths. A similar point can be made about mediation. Police specials and probation volunteers, on the other hand, may each be involved in work with juveniles at risk. Equally, victim support volunteers, police specials and perhaps also probation volunteers could have a part to play in neighbourhood watch. Whilst integration to the agency may be an important factor behind volunteer morale, it should not be taken to the extremes which often reflect official relationships between, say, the police and probation services. Moreover, as we have stressed already, integration of volunteers tends to weaken volunteers' status as *community* participants.

THE LIMITS TO INTEGRATION

So far we have focused on the advantages of integrating volunteers. We have left unchallenged the notion that there are inherent problems. Yet clearly there are. For example, we have discussed the benefits of volunteers for local accountability. This is particularly the case when they work amongst professionals and therefore are exposed to working practices. In these circumstances as Morris (1969) has contended, volunteers are in a position to publicize malpractices. However, our evidence suggests that some volunteers, for example, some specials, do not adopt this stance as a matter of course. Indeed we uncovered examples where specials themselves broke rules in pursuit of police objectives. The key issue here is that successful integration of the volunteer into the agency may negate any potential benefit from wider accountability. So how can over-identification, largely in the interests of employees, be controlled?

Let us consider the example of police volunteers. The objective of any policy would be to encourage specials to see themselves less as (part-time) police officers, and more as volunteers. One idea would be to 'distance' specials from regulars; perhaps by changing the uniform so that it was strikingly different from regulars. Unfortunately this has been tried before (see Gill 1986b; 1987) and caused confusion amongst the public who mistook specials for bus inspectors and traffic wardens. At the same time it caused much annoyance amongst police volunteers. So it is a policy that has been tried and already failed.

It will be recalled that the specials were integrated into the police because of ongoing training, the ready availability of work, and the socialization opportunities. In this chapter we have argued that other agencies might adopt the same in order to integrate their voluntary workers. Clearly we would not now recommend limiting these policies to prevent over-identification. Nevertheless, there is perhaps more to commend a joint training package in order that specials could understand the volunteer role in addition to that of a police officer.

In reality, of course, if volunteers adopt the role of public spies there is a danger, even a likelihood, that they will be shunned by professionals, and excluded altogether. There are perhaps four points which need to be stressed here. First, any policy which encourages specials to identify less with the police service will at the same time thwart their integration. Second, as confirmed, infractions of the rules were not common, and specials were no more likely to circumvent rules, and probably much less likely to do so, than were regulars. Third, in reality, if a special reported a regular, and for that matter another special, it would require corroboration which was not always available. Fourth, if a special did report a regular officer, it would probably reflect badly on the specials as a group and result in widespread rejection of the police volunteer, and ultimately no public participation at all.

In all then the public may have a price to pay for fully integrated volunteers. There is a danger though of artificially inflating the price. Certainly there are advantages for the public in having more people informed about police practices; and it is perhaps even encouraging that specials considered that police illegalities were rare. Given the potential advantages of fully integrated volunteers, not least in terms of resources, and the relative unlikelihood of many volunteers witnessing serious irregularities and not bringing them to wider attention, the price is indeed a small one. However, it would not be in the public interest to pay specials and thereby encourage them to view themselves as semi-professionals.

SUMMARY

In this chapter we have discussed a number of issues relevant to organizing volunteers. It has never been our intention to construct a comprehensive model for organizing volunteers. Rather we are keen to highlight and discuss the implications of certain policies. We have done this against a background of the type of organization to which it applied.

It has been shown that the nature of the police organization made it more conductive to integrating volunteers. The uniform and availability of work built up an identity; ongoing training and socialization assisted the process. These benefits did not exist for probation volunteers. Victim-support volunteers suffered from a paucity of work, aggravated by the location of key gatekeepers in a separate organization; at the same time victim support was in many areas very new and still aiming to establish an identity. Whilst we would not suggest that other volunteers should wear uniforms, it is nonetheless true that many procedures which presently operate within the police might be applied successfully elsewhere. Volunteers can be better organized and deployed so as to demonstrate their value to the agency.

Initially though we expressed concern that the much discussed 'typical volunteer' might be a direct result of agency selection procedures. Hence it was suggested that agencies should consider the part that screening processes may play in perpetuating biases. This is not a call for more relaxed or more rigorous selection processes; merely a concern that discussions of who is a volunteer should not be divorced from discussions of agency policy. Equally volunteers should be recruited with a clear rationale – of what is required of them and who might appropriately 'fit the bill'.

Part of the reason why this issue has remained unrecognized, or at least received very scant commentary, is because professionals, and agencies generally, remain ignorant of issues relating to volunteering. Volunteers are still a neglected part of professional training. It is unlikely that concerted attempts to integrate and utilize volunteers can realistically take place against a background of professional and agency ignorance.

Thus, while we argue that professionals should be involved in the various stages of the volunteer process, including the training and co-ordinating of volunteers, we realize that at present there will be limits to possible benefits. Professionals do not recognize the importance of volunteers, and they are not encouraged by organizations to allocate sufficient time to volunteer issues. Still it remains our belief that they should.

What has emerged is the considerable part agencies can play in integrating volunteers. Opportunities to socialize even at regular meetings and training sessions are important; the provision of work is crucial. Indeed more volunteers could and should be advised of the expectations of them, and notice taken of their needs and ambitions on their induction into the agency. Unused volunteers can prove an anathema to the agency, expressing unfavourable rather than benign comments amongst the general public. There are numerous other ways in which volunteers can be made to feel wanted, and there is much scope here for developing initiatives.

We have outlined some potential benefits in a joint training programme. Here we noted the opportunity for people to learn about issues relating to volunteering. This may be of particular importance to the specials given the problem we noted there of over-identification. At the same time though, while accepting that over-identification does exist, there is a danger of the disadvantages being exaggerated. Of particular concern is the likelihood that potential remedies would thwart the integration of volunteers. This would be of benefit to no one. Rather we prefer to suggest that over-identification is a small price the public might have to pay for the integration of volunteers, where volunteer morale is high and use is maximized. This, of course, does not apply to volunteers, such as those in lay visitor schemes, who are explicitly recruited to enhance accountability and wider public control. However, where this is not the case there is no point in pretending that volunteers can profitably be used to increase accountability. Realistically they cannot.

In all, volunteers can be a valuable addition to agencies. At present the value is scarcely realized. In this chapter we have tried to identify some issues for policy makers. Regardless of organizational type, there are lessons to be learnt on the ways in which volunteers can be integrated. Our findings may be a pathfinder to achieving that objective.

8 | CONCLUSIONS

SUMMARY AND DISCUSSION

At the start of this text we attempted to outline the role played by the public in the criminal-justice system. It was shown that, while both the control of order, and provision of welfare were once the responsibility of the family and the community, industrialized society saw a move towards state control. We noted that similar developments occurred abroad. However, as the state expanded, so its limitations were realized, and some community involvement has been seen to become either desirable or necessary. But what form of community involvement? Here we have concentrated on the voluntary sector, but this is clearly a heterogeneous category.

We attempted to tackle this in more detail in Chapter 2 by looking specifically at the voluntary sector. We discussed the definitional problems, complicated by the range of roles played by voluntary groups and the functions undertaken by them. Notwithstanding the difficulties outlined, we suggested four criteria by which we can begin to distinguish – although not exclusively – between different organizations: the relationship between the voluntary agency and state services; source of funding; goals; the relationship between helper and helped.

Of course distinguishing between voluntary organizations is a very different task from distinguishing between volunteers, and hence we offered a different typology for this purpose. Leaving aside the relationship between helper and helped which overlapped the typology for organizations, we identified five dimensions by which volunteers and their work can be classified: status, power, role, intra-agency specialism and work programme. Through this we hoped to have illustrated the range of tasks and range of meanings attached to the work undertaken by volunteers. We would thus argue that to talk about volunteers in isolation from an organization context runs the risk, at the very least, of simplicity.

From here we moved on to consider, on a general level, some of the advantages and problems of the voluntary sector, both in terms of the organization and the volunteer. The benefits include the provision of service variety and quality, presenting as it does competition to the state. Volunteers and voluntary organizations are also pioneers, uncovering new needs and attempting to meet them, with victim-support schemes being but one recent example. That the voluntary sector can act as a pressure group to instigate change or highlight injustices, where it provides an independent voice, is clearly also beneficial. At the same time we suggested that giving freely was a core element of a good society, enabling each to participate; not only overcoming some shortcomings of state bureaucracies but at the same time fulfilling an ingredient of democracy.

Perhaps inevitably there are disadvantages too. We identified a few, including the potential threat volunteers pose to professionals, their unreliability and the ecological imbalance. On a different level we noted that some benefits can, from a different perspective, be seen as problems. The role of volunteers offering help on the same level as the client is illustrated by the unrepresentativeness of volunteers generally. Similarly, the greater reliance on state funding, we noted, does bring into question the extent to which voluntary organizations can be seen as independent.

In Chapters 3, 4 and 5 we went on to consider some of these issues in the specific context of, respectively, probation, police and victim support. In each case we commenced with an historical introduction where the very different histories were outlined. Specials were known to have roots in the seventeenth century and expanded throughout the early eighteenth century. By contrast probation volunteers of the late nineteenth century and early twentieth century gave way to employed officers and then professionals, but re-entered the stage in the 1960s. Victim support, however, is of far more recent development, from its humble beginnings in the 1970s.

When we went on to consider the international stage, we noticed many parallels between countries in the part played by volunteers. In Britain there does appear to be greater national co-ordination but, with some notable exceptions, it would be difficult to argue that this country is any less (or for that matter more) community spirited then most others. Most important though was the impression that much could be gained from a greater international comparison, not only of volunteers but also of the agencies that deploy them.

From here we moved on to consider the situation nationally, and in each agency the idea of voluntarism appears to be thriving. This is particularly the case in victim support which is growing steadily and appears highly committed to the volunteer principle despite increased funding from the state. In the police there has been a reduction in the number of specials, although this is partly due to a change of policy, from earlier days when specials would be expected to attend but one function a year, to a more formalized structure today. Still it appears that, while commitment to the specials is most apparent at central-government level and indeed at senior-officer level, there is more scepticism amongst the junior ranks. In the probation service too, although volunteers were used in a variety of imaginative tasks, services suffered from a lack of commitment in practice by some officers.

These points were reiterated in our review of the role of volunteers in the South-west. Here, at least, the majority of volunteers in each agency were under-employed, yet the amount of work that could be undertaken varied both within and between agencies. In probation it depended obviously not only on the number of cases officers were prepared to refer, but also with the type of task. Those working in day centres could rarely claim insufficient work. Likewise those involved in ongoing casework frequently lamented the lack of opportunities. In the specials the means by which people became involved varied. Thus some stations simply required specials on a rota basis, for example, for two sessions a month on every Friday night. At other stations involvement depended on the special constable indicating when he or she wanted to go on duty, at others specials had to wait to be asked. In victim support there was simply a lack of referrals from the police, a problem which was accentuated where an indirect, rather than a direct referral policy operated.

Comparing the volunteers within each agency proved a most interesting task, and this we attempted in Chapter 6. We focused on a number of variables concerning volunteers, their ideologies and motivations. In looking at motivations we stressed that asking someone why he or she wanted to undertake voluntary work was different from asking about choice of a particular agency. Some probation volunteers but rather more specials noted that the two questions were entwined and that they had volunteered to work with one specific agency. Overall, there was rather less emphasis on the philanthropic motive than Wolfenden (1978) suggests. We found more volunteers were inspired by self-directed reasons, although in probation this took the form of career reasons. This was also accentuated in the context of why probation volunteers chose to work with the probation service at least compared to specials and victim-support volunteers, where organizational reasons and drift were more evident in accounting for choice of agency.

The drift effect, we argued, is crucial to any consideration of why people volunteer. It is not detached from considerations of the word-of-mouth recruitment tool: many volunteer simply because they are approached by a representative of the agency, and so drift into work with that agency. This in turn will account, along with organizational selection procedures, for who finally gets elected, a point, though perhaps obvious, which is certainly not sufficiently stressed in the literature. Certainly it was possible to distinguish between volunteers with the different organizations. Specials were mainly males with views which might more generally be cast as right of centre. Victim support contained mainly older people and housewives, partly because of their availability during the day. Probation volunteers were the more eclectic group, correspondingly involved in a wider variety of tasks. On an ideological level, we found specials to adopt a more authoritarian line in contrast to probation volunteers; specials saw the crime problem as severe, as did victim-support volunteers, but the latter aligned with probation volunteers in being more closely identified with treatment solutions. At this point we linked the ideology of the volunteers with those of the organization in which they worked and noted the possibility that volunteer subcultures might emerge. Such subcultures, we suggested, are important in a number of respects, but their formation is dependent on a variety of factors which the agency can influence. This was the focus of Chapter 7. Here we looked at the role of the professional policies of recruiting and selecting, training and co-ordinating and deploying volunteers. In addition, we raised the problem of over-identification, of crucial importance in the context of volunteer cultures as equivalents to occupational cultures.

We drew attention to the important part professionals must play in effective volunteer deployment. This is true regardless of whether volunteers are in the same agency like police and probation, or a separate one like victim support. In our view the move towards professionalization has discouraged proper consideration of the lay contribution; the lack of attention to volunteers in professional training is testament to this. We are aware that this is not a new observation and reflects the traditional neglect of volunteers. Professionals must, however, because of the values, as well as the problems associated with the use of volunteers, be taught how best to encourage the volunteer potential.

Scepticism of volunteers is frequently based on misunderstandings, or a lack of understanding, for example, about why someone should want to undertake tasks without financial reward. Training should incorporate this. Similarly professionals sometimes lament the fact that volunteers are 'the wrong type' without an awareness of the part played by organizational recruitment and selection policies in perpetuating those biases.

Improved understanding will also result if professionals are more closely involved in co-ordinating volunteers and, in particular, if a person with the status of a professional is given a central role, recognizing the value of volunteers to an organization. We also suggested that there is greater scope for incorporating the service of ex-professionals as volunteers, where knowledge and skills could be retained to the benefit of all concerned.

In the American literature there has been talk of volunteers having rights. While at the present time to formalize rights in a British context would be to risk further isolation from already sceptical professionals, it nevertheless remains true that volunteers should have certain conditions met. The provision of a training programme is a case in point. Hence we argued that the benefits extend beyond the provision of skills to make them more effective in their volunteer task, most especially by providing volunteers with an attachment to the agency and with a feeling that they are valued. At the same time it provides an opportunity for agencies to inculcate volunteers with expectation of how they operate and the agency culture. Building up a service of commitment is vital for an effective volunteer culture.

At the very best volunteers needed to be provided with work. Many volunteers we spoke to were under-employed. Clearly there is a danger these people will express a jaundiced view of the organization and one of the potential benefits of using volunteers quickly turns into a disadvantage. Involvement encourages commitment which creates a healthy voluntary-work environment.

At this point we need to stress caution. We have built up a picture of volunteers being actively engaged in the work of the organization, properly prepared, and being identified with the perceived ideology of the organization. There is a problem though of over-identification where, for example, the specials were prepared to circumvent guidelines to pursue police objectives. If we consider that one potential role for volunteers is that of opening up statutory agencies and making them more accountable to the community, then the specials' over-identification is indeed problematic. Further discussion, however, showed that policies to rectify this would only isolate specials altogether. Hence we noted that there were limits to this expectation. For other reasons it was unrealistic. Instead we suggested a need to rely on common sense; some volunteers would, where possible, report misdemeanours and so, we would hope, would other professionals. So, while on the one hand we point to the other advantages of volunteers, we in addition see benefits in a joint training programme, whereby people could learn the role volunteers can play in general, in addition to specific aspects relevant to their work. Also, since some volunteers drift into work with an agency, it may be they are not in an agency whose work best suits them. Joint training would inform and help to rectify this possible dilemma and, given the pooling of resources, might ultimately benefit the hard-pressed voluntary sector.

To this extent, this study has hopefully suggested that, despite the multifarious tasks undertaken by volunteers, there are a number of key similarities. It does appear that these similarities extend to the international stage too. Thus it may be possible to theorize about volunteering to a greater extent than has been attempted by our own limited study. What is crucial, and this we hope is clear, is that studies of volunteering must not exclude the organizational context, in particular organizational policies which can serve to enrich or thwart the volunteer contribution.

WHERE DO WE GO FROM HERE?

We are not the first researchers to identify different volunteers in different organizations according to the different expectations of rewards in voluntary work, as contributions to Hatch's (1982) volume testifies. However, we would argue that our approach marks a new stage in volunteer research in assessing the interaction between motivations, deployment and organizational policies. However, it does display a number of limitations.

During the course of our research we have noted that, as volunteers become more immersed in the organization, so they are more affected by agency policies, and so distinct differences begin to emerge along organizational lines. However, it has not been possible to trace these changes over time and we would thus highlight advantages in a longitudinal study to rectify this deficiency.

Just as important, it remains to be shown whether similar observations can be made about other volunteer groups in other contexts. Presently the many good studies on neighbourhood watch have excluded considerations of volunteers' motivations and ideologies, a point which we hope current research in the South-west will rectify. Similarly in the Health Service a range of volunteer groups are identifiable undertaking a variety of tasks. The uniformed St John Ambulance is quite markedly distinct from Age Concern, as they both are from hospital radio. We would hope more research might incorporate a comparative dimension along the lines we have pursued.

Of course there is a distinct difference between conducting research, noting relevant findings, and obtaining action to rectify deficiencies uncovered. We hope our text is a contribution to improving the treatment of volunteers and of realizing the potential advantages organized volunteers can bring. While recent experience suggests that such a time may yet be a distant one, the increasing reliance on the voluntary sector and the growing awareness of limitations of statutory provisions suggest that it cannot be too soon and indeed may already be too late. If the time is not yet ripe for alarmist comments, then it is ripe for action, not only because it may encourage an improvement to the system, but because it is so blatantly linked to common sense.

NOTES

CHAPTER 2

1 For a fuller discussion of the voluntary–statutory partnership see Brenton (1985). A useful review of current problems facing the voluntary sector is contained in *Community Care*, 25 February 1988.

2 Probation volunteers are sometimes known as voluntary associates, or VAs. To avoid confusion, we have used the term probation volunteers throughout, although our respondents have not always done so. They are normally accredited (i.e. officially approved and registered by the service) although there are some unaccredited volunteers, and the ratio of accredited to unaccredited volunteers varies in different services. Our sampling frame is restricted to accredited volunteers only, it being the policy (if not always practice – see note 6 of Chapter 3) in both counties to accredit all volunteers where possible.

3 At the time of the research there were 14 schemes operating in the two counties. One, which had a mixed relationship with NAVSS, refused to co-operate in the research; the remaining scheme co-operated with us to some extent but its volunteers were not included in the samples.

CHAPTER 3

1 The US situation is confused in a number of respects which make direct comparisons difficult. For example, there is a federal service and state-based services, and other agencies are also involved with services like parole which in Britain are part of the probation service

2 Probation in Sweden is both community- and institution-based. Probation officers act as administrators/supervisors with volunteers, who are paid 'expenses', providing most direct contact with clients.

3 See note 2 to Chapter 2.

4 SOVA, the Society of Voluntary Associates, is a London-based organization which specializes in recruiting and training volunteers for the probation service. It also provides a variety of services for probation services elsewhere in the country.

5 Some services may well have included this under the heading 'general enquiries from the public'.

6 Details here are based only on accredited volunteers. We did, however, discover in the course of our research that one section of Devon tended to accredit rather fewer of its volunteers than did the others. The result of this 'statistical deficiency' was to minimize inter-constituency correlations.

7 Usually volunteers were advised not to offer loans to clients, although many did and most appeared to have been repaid. One volunteer who lent £30 – which was considered a large amount – to a client was severely reprimanded by a probation officer.

8 For a full discussion of motivations see Gill (1986b). We have used the terms 'other-directed' and 'self-directed' in place of altruism and egoism, not least because the former sounds patronizing and the latter pejorative. Indeed, the definitions of each are problematic. We have used 'drift' to refer to those volunteers who did not make a determined decision to volunteer, but instead became involved because of other influences.

9 This finding does, of course, raise the possibility that respondents might have been unrepresentative. Certainly, a danger of postal surveys is that those who are indifferent or inexperienced in the area will not reply.

CHAPTER 4

1 Seth's (1961: 34) reference to an Act of 1673, which is often quoted, is, in fact, incorrect.

2 It is, however, still possible for police authorities to pay specials in addition to reimbursing expenses.

3 These and subsequent examples not otherwise referenced are based on replies by the forces in question to our enquiries.

4 It should, however, be noted that hours worked by specials could have been slightly inflated over the research period which coincided with the miners' strike.

5 At the time of the research only applicants who had not obtained the minimum educational qualifications were required to sit the test and the pass mark was slightly lower than for applicants to the regulars. This has now been changed, and all applicants to the specials must sit the test and obtain the same pass mark as is required for entrance to the regulars.

6 Clearly, as we have noted elsewhere (Mawby and Gill 1987) the more positive attitude of probation officers is to some extent the result of their exposure to the perspectives of social-policy specialists.

CHAPTER 5

1 Based on discussions with K. Hannaford. The federal system in Australia, as in Canada, has meant that service initiatives vary considerably between different provinces or states.

2 Figures are only approximate, given that the ways in which local schemes record cases on a monthly basis sometimes results in referrals being double-counted.

3 As we have noted elsewhere (Mawby and Gill 1987) this has been a source of much dispute nationally, although rural schemes with relatively fewer crime referrals, like many in the South-west, have maintained a commitment to non-crime referrals.

4 Based on discussions with Gill Roxborough.

5 Based on discussions with Susan Sagar, Mark Williams and Richard Miller. See also Birmingham Victim Support, B Division, *Eighth Annual Report 1986/87*. Under the new Employment Training initiative this alternative has been limited. See ibid., *Tenth Annual Report 1988/89*.

6 Discussed in panel sessions or at the NAVSS annual conferences, University of Warwick, 1988 and 1989, and currently the subject of a Home Office funded research initiative.

CHAPTER 6

1 The figures for self-directed reasons would then be as follows: voluntary associates 48 per cent; specials 47 per cent, victim-support volunteers 42 per cent.

2 The Constitution requires schemes to have a representative of either church *or* voluntary agency on the Management Committee.

3 There is a growing trend of encouraging people to join the specials before embarking on a career. At the same time some applicants who fail the police entrance test are directed to the specials. Thus we would expect a greater emphasis on career motivations in future studies of the specials.

4 We fully appreciate that by evaluating career reasons as part of the 'other-directed' category in the initial decision to volunteer and part of 'organization' here, we could be accused of playing with statistics. In part our problem is that categories are not mutually exclusive. However, the type of replies we received to the two questions were qualitatively different. That so many qualified their answer with a mention of the probation service encourages us to make a link here.

5 It could be argued that there exists some therapeutic benefit in running a football team as group work. Or alternatively transporting clients to court affords the opportunity to meet and gain the confidence of a client or to gain necessary information or to discuss any problems or whatever. The point that is being made here is that training may be more important for some tasks than for others.

6 Gay and Hatch (1983) make the point that agencies will have to take positive action to increase the involvement of the unemployed. One of the key features in discussion groups at the BASW conference on volunteers, held in Birmingham on 2 July 1987 to promote the BASW publication (Ridley and Currie 1987), was the role of unemployed volunteers. A number of commentators noted that unemployed volunteers were becoming increasingly common, but they brought with them additional demands, particularly in wanting to give a lot more time. Apparently, some agencies had found it difficult to adjust to these needs!

7 The choice was not offered to the other two samples. Nevertheless high ranking by victim-support volunteers seems to indicate a distinctive quality here.

8 It needs to be borne in mind that Devon and Cornwall is a largely Conservative area but with a good Liberal tradition. The probation-volunteer support for Labour is well above the average for the two counties as a whole.

CHAPTER 7

1 A whole range of information sheets helpful to charities, voluntary organizations, volunteers and agencies using volunteers is available for a modest charge, from the Volunteer Centre, 29 Lower Kings Road, Berkhamsted, Herts, H84 2AB.

2 Some volunteers did meet the police on a regular basis. Volunteers who sat on the committee are a case in point. This, of course, applied to only a few.

3 Not all specials would accept this, particularly those who were underworked or wanted to engage in more varied or taxing duties. But specials were not inactive, and from an objective viewpoint, and certainly compared with probation volunteers and victim-support volunteers, specials were integrated into the police.

4 SOVA claim to have employed this method successfully.

5 Co-ordinators in this study had time because of the lack of referrals. It certainly would not be true of schemes generally.

BIBLIOGRAPHY

Alderson, J. C. (1978). 'Concepts of preventive policing', in *The Cranfield Papers*. London: Peel Press.

Alderson, J. C. (1979). *Policing Freedom*. Plymouth, Macdonald and Evans.

Alderson, J. C. (1981a). 'Hong Kong, Tokyo, Peking: three police systems observed'. *Police Studies*, 3.4, 3–12.

Alderson, J. C. (1981b). 'The cause for community policing'. Submission to Scarman Inquiry.

Ames, W. L. (1979). 'Police in the community'. *Police Journal*, 52, 252–9.

Ames, W. L. (1981). *Police and Community in Japan*. Berkeley, University of California Press.

Anderson, D. (1981). *Breaking the Spell of the Welfare State*. London, Social Affairs Unit.

Armstrong, M. (1967). 'The campaign against parasites', in P. H. Juviler and H. W. Morton (eds). *Soviet Policy-Makers*. New York, Praeger.

Aves, G. (1969). *Voluntary Workers in the Social Services*. London, Allen & Unwin/BASW.

Bailey, V. (1981). 'Introduction' in V. Bailey (ed.). *Policing and Punishment in Nineteenth-Century Britain*. London, Croom Helm.

Baillie, D. (1967). 'Charlie come home'. *Probation*, 13.2, 36–41.

Baker, R. and Baker, J. (1966). 'The role and potential value of volunteers in social defence'. *International Review of Criminal Policy*, part 1, 69–72.

Baldwin, J. (1976). 'The social composition of the magistracy'. *British Journal of Criminology*, 16, 171–4.

Baldwin, J. and McConville, M. (1979). *Jury Trials*. London, Oxford University Press.

Bankowski, Z. K., Hutton, N. R. and McManus, J. J. (1987). *Lay Justice?* Edinburgh, T. and T. Clarke.

Banton, M. (1973). *Police Community Relations*. London, Collins.

Barclay, P. M. (1982). *Social Workers: Their Role and Tasks*. London, Bedford Square Press.

Barr, H. (1971). *Volunteers in Prison After-Care*. London, Allen & Unwin.

Bayley, D. H. (1976). *Forces of Order: Police Behaviour in Japan and the United States.* Berkeley, University of California Press.

Bayley, D. H. (1985). *Patterns of Policing: A Comparative International Analysis.* New Brunswick, Rutgers University Press.

Becker, H. K. and Hjellemo, E. O. (1976). *Justice in Modern Sweden.* Springfield, Illinois, Thomas.

Bennett, T. (1987). 'Neighbourhood watch: principles and practices', in R. I. Mawby (ed.). *Policing Britain.* Plymouth, Plymouth Polytechnic.

Berg, B. L. and Doerner, W. G. (1987). 'Volunteer police officers: an unexamined personnel dimension in law enforcement'. Paper to American Society of Criminology Conference, Montreal.

Berman, J. (1969). 'The Cuban popular tribunals'. *Columbia Law Review*, 69, 1317–54.

Beveridge, Lord and Wells, A. F. (1949). *The Evidence for Voluntary Action.* Connecticut, Greenwood Press.

Binns, P. and Gonzalez, M. (1980). 'Cuba, Castro and socialism'. *International Socialism*, series 2 (8), 1–36.

Blacher, M. (1989). 'Living on the margins: nightshelter use and single homelessness in a British city'. Ph.D. thesis. Plymouth, Plymouth Polytechnic.

Blair, I. (1985). *Investigating Rape.* Beckenham, Croom Helm.

Bohart, P. H. (1977). 'A viable police reserve'. *FBI Law Enforcement*, 46, February, 9–15.

Bolin, D. C. (1980). 'The Pima County victim witness program: analysing its success'. *Evaluating Change*, special issue, 120–6.

Bottomley, A. K. and Coleman, C. (1981). *Understanding Crime Rates.* Aldershot, Gower.

Bottoms, A. E. and McWilliams, W. (1979). 'A non-treatment paradigm for probation practice'. *British Journal of Social Work*, 9, 159–202.

Bottoms, A. E., Mawby, R. I. and Walker, M. (1987). 'A localised crime survey in contrasting areas of a city'. *British Journal of Criminology*, 27, 125–54.

Brasnett, M. (1969). *Voluntary Social Action.* London, National Council of Social Service.

Brenton, M. (1985). *The Voluntary Sector in British Social Services.* London, Longman.

Brogden, M. (1987). 'The emergence of the police: the colonial dimension'. *British Journal of Criminology*, 27, 4–15.

Brogden, M., Jefferson, T. and Walklate, S. (1988). *Introducing Policework.* London, Unwin Hyman.

Brown, R. M. (1969a). 'Historical patterns of violence in America', in H. D. Graham and T. R. Gurr (eds). *The History of Violence in America.* New York, Praeger.

Brown, R. M. (1969b). 'The American vigilante tradition', in H. D. Graham and T. R. Gurr (eds). *The History of Violence in America.* New York, Praeger.

Burrows, J., Ekblom, P. and Heal, K. (1979). *Crime Prevention and the Police.* London, HMSO (HORS no. 55).

Byrne, J. M. (1987). 'Evaluating the effectiveness of the "new" intermediate sanctions: a nationwide review of intensified community correction programs'. Paper to American Society of Criminology Conference, Montreal.

Cain, M. (1963). *Society and the Policeman's Role.* London, Routledge & Kegan Paul.

Central Statistical Office (1986). *Social Trends.* London, HMSO.

Central Statistical Office (1988). *Social Trends.* London, HMSO.

Clarke, A. T. (1977). *Volunteers Accredited to the Probation Service.* Hertford, Hertfordshire Probation and After Care Service (Supplement 70).

Clifford, W. (1976). *Crime Control in Japan*. Lexington, Mass., Lexington.

Cohen, J. A. (1968). *The Criminal Process in the People's Republic of China, 1949–1963*. Cambridge, Mass., Harvard University Press.

Cohen, J. A. (1971). 'Drafting people's meditation rules', in J. W. Lewis (ed.). *The City in Communist China*. Stanford, Calif., Stanford University Press.

Colver, A. (1969). 'CSV with the Liverpool Probation Service'. *Probation*, 15.2, 71–2.

Cooper, J. and Pomeyie, J. (1988). 'Racial attacks and racial harassment: lessons from a local project', in M. Maguire and J. Pointing (eds). *Victims of Crime*. Milton Keynes, Open University Press.

Corbett, C. and Hobdell, K. (1988). 'Volunteer-based services to rape victims: some recent developments', in M. Maguire and J. Pointing (eds). *Victims of Crime*. Milton Keynes, Open University Press.

Critchley, T. A. (1978). *A History of Police in England and Wales*. London, Constable.

Darvill, G. (1975). *Bargain or Barricade?* Berkhamsted, Volunteer Centre.

Davidson, V., Goss, C. and Davidson, N. (1985). *Volunteers Survey 1983: Final Report*. Hull, Humberside Probation Service.

Davis, G., Boucherat, J. and Watson, D. (1987). *A Preliminary Study of Victim Offender Mediation and Reparation Schemes*. London, HMSO (HORPU paper no. 42).

Deacon, B. (1983). *Social Policy and Socialism*. London, Pluto Press.

Deitch, L. I. and Thompson, L. N. (1985). 'The reserve police officer: one alternative to the need for manpower'. *Police Chief*, 52, May, 59–61.

Devlin, P. (1956). *Trial by Jury*. London, Methuen.

Donoghoe, M., Dorn, N., James, C., Jones, S., Ribbens, J. and South, N. (1987). 'How families and communities respond to heroin', in N. Dorn and N. South (eds). *A Land Fit For Heroin?* Basingstoke, Macmillan.

Dowell, D. A. (1978). 'Volunteers in probation: a research note on evaluation'. *Journal of Criminal Justice*, 6, 357–61.

Ellenbogen, J. and Digregorio, B. (1975). 'Volunteers in probation: exploring new dimensions'. *Judicature*, 58, 6, 281–5.

Emsley, C. (1983). *Policing and its Context, 1750–1870*. London, Macmillan.

Ericson, R. V., McMahon, M. W. and Evans, D. G. (1987). 'Punishing for profit: reflections on the revival of privatization in corrections'. *Canadian Journal of Criminology*, 29, 355–88.

Erwin, B. S. and Bennett, L. A. (1987). 'New dimensions in probation: Georgia's experience with intensive probation supervision (IPS)'. National Institute of Justice, Research in Brief, US Department of Justice.

Eskridge, C. W. and Carlson, E. W. (1979). 'The use of volunteers in probation: a national synthesis'. *Journal of Offender Counselling, Services and Rehabilitation*, 4, 175–89.

Etzioni, A. (1961). *A Comparative Analysis of Complex Organization*. New York, Free Press.

Etzioni, A. (1969). *The Semi-Professions and their Organization: Teachers, Nurses, Social Workers*. New York, Free Press.

Fielding, N. (1988). *Joining Forces*. London, Routledge.

Figgie Report (1983). *Reducing Crime in America: Part IV: Successful Community Efforts*.

Findlay, M. and Duff, P. (eds) (1988). *The Jury Under Attack*. London, Butterworth.

Fo, W. S. and O'Donnell, C. R. (1974). 'The buddy system: relationship and contingency ambitions in a community intervention program for youth with non professionals as behaviour change agents'. *Journal of Consulting and Clinical Psychology*, 42, 163–9.

Fo, W. S. and O'Donnell, C. R. (1975). 'The buddy system: effect of community intervention on delinquent offences'. *Behaviour Therapy*, 6, 522–4.

Foster, P. (1983). *Access to Welfare*. London, Macmillan.

Frantz, J. B. (1969). 'The frontier tradition: an invitation to violence', in H. D. Graham and T. R. Gourr (eds). *The History of Violence in America*. New York, Praeger.

Fry, M. (1951). *Arms of the Law*. London, Victor Gollancz.

Fulcher, J. (1988). 'The bureaucratization of the state and the rise of Japan'. *British Journal of Sociology*, 39, 288–54.

Fyfe, N. (1987). 'Contesting consultation'. Paper to British Criminology Conference, Sheffield.

Gandy, J. M. (1977). 'Volunteers in four provincial adult organizational institutions: services provided and perceptions of staff'. *Canadian Journal of Criminology and Corrections*, 19, 67–79.

Gay, P. and Hatch, S. (1983). *Voluntary Work and Unemployment*. Sheffield Policy Studies Institute, Research and Development Series 15. Manpower Services Commission.

Gill, M. L. (1986a). 'Wife battering: a case study of a women's refuge', in R. I. Mawby (ed.). *Crime Victims*. Plymouth, Plymouth Polytechnic.

Gill, M. L. (1986b). 'Voluntarism and the Criminal Justice System: a Comparative Analysis'. Ph.D. thesis. Plymouth, Plymouth Polytechnic.

Gill, M. L. (1987). 'The special constabulary: community representation and accountability', in R. I. Mawby (ed.). *Policing Britain*. Plymouth, Plymouth Polytechnic.

Gill, M. L. and Andrews, M. (1987). 'Results find volunteers use receives little priority during training'. *Social Work Today*, 11 May, 7–8.

Gill, M. L. and Mawby, R. I. (1990). *A Special Kind of Constable?* Aldershot, Avebury.

Gittler, J. (1984). 'Expanding the role of the victim in a criminal action: an overview of issues and problems'. *Pepperdine Law Review*, 11, 117–82.

Goddard, J. and Jacobson, G. (1967). 'Volunteer services in a juvenile court'. *Crime and Delinquency*, 13, 336–43.

Gourley, D. and Bristow, A. P. (1970). *Patrol Administration*. Springfield, Charles C. Thomas.

Greenberg, M. A. (1978). 'Auxiliary civilian police – the New York City experience'. *Journal of Police Science and Administration*, 6, 86–97.

Greenwood, P. and Chaiken, J. (1977). *The Crime Investigation Process*. Lexington, Mass., D. C. Heath.

Griffiths, P. (1971). *To Guard my People: the History of the Indian Police*. London, Ernest Benn.

Hadley, R. and Scott, M. (1980). *Time to Give? Retired People as Volunteers*. Berkhamsted, Volunteer Centre.

Hardiker, P. (1977). 'Social work ideologies in the probation service'. *British Journal of Social Work*, 4, 131–54.

Harding, J. (1982). *Victims and Offenders: Needs and Responsibilities*. London, NCVO, Bedford Square Press.

Hart, J. (1955). 'Reform of the borough police, 1835–1856'. *English Historical Review*, 70, 411–27.

Hart, J. (1956). 'The County and Borough Police Act, 1856'. *Public Administration*, 34, 405–17.

Hatch, S. (1980). *Outside the State*. London, Bedford Square Press.

Hatch, S. (ed.) (1982). *Volunteers: Patterns, Meanings and Motives*. Berkhamsted, Volunteer Centre.

Hatch, S. and Mocroft, I. (1977). 'Factors affecting the location of voluntary organization branches'. *Policy and Politics*, 6, 163–72.

Haxby, D. (1978). *Probation: a Changing Service*. London, Constable.

Heidenheimer, A. J., Heclo, H. and Adams, T. C. (1983). *Comparative Public Policy: the Politics of Choice in Europe and America*. London, Macmillan.

Hess, A. G. (1970). 'The volunteer probation officers of Japan'. *International Journal of Offender Therapy*, 14, 8–14.

Hill, J. (1981). *The Use of Volunteers by West Midlands Probation and After Care Service*. Birmingham, West Midlands Probation and After Care Service.

Hoare, M. (1988). 'Post Office "Eyes" go private'. *Policy Review*, 18 March, 592–3.

Hobhouse, R. (1939). *Benjamin Waugh: Founder of the NSPCC and Framer of the 'Children's Charter'*. London, Daniel.

Hogg, D. (1988). 'A "special" relationship'. *Police Review*, 19 February, 378–9.

Holdaway, S. (1983). *Inside the British Police: a Force at Work*. Oxford, Blackwell.

Holdaway, S. (1986). 'Police and social work relations – problems and possibilities?' *British Journal of Social Work*, 16, 137–60.

Holme, A. and Maizels, J. (1978). *Social Workers and Volunteers*. London, Allen & Unwin/BASW.

Holtom, C. and Raynor, P. (1988). 'Origins of victims support philosophy and practice', in M. Maguire and J. Pointing (eds). *Victims of Crime*. Milton Keynes, Open University Press.

Home Office (1984). 'Probation service in England and Wales: statement of national objectives and priorities'. Home Office, April (mimeo).

Home Office (1986). *Criminal Statistics for England and Wales*. London, HMSO.

Home Office (1987). *Report of the Conference on Special Constables on 7 December 1987*. London, HMSO (mimeo).

Home Office (1988). *Report of Her Majesty's Chief Inspector of Constabulary, 1987*. London, HMSO.

Hood, R. (1972). *Sentencing the Motoring Offender*. London, Heinemann.

Hope, R. and Lloyd, T. (1984). *Commissioners' Action Plan 1/9/84: Increase Recruitment to the MSC*. London, Metropolitan Police (mimeo).

Horejsi, C. R. (1971). 'Parents' perception of the effect of volunteers in juvenile probation'. Ph.D. thesis. University of Denver (School of Social Work).

Horejsi, C. R. (1973). 'Training for the direct-service volunteer in probation'. *Federal Probation*, 37.3, 38–41.

Hough, M. and Mayhew, P. (1985). *Taking Account of Crime: Key Findings from the 1984 British Crime Survey*. London, HMSO (HORS no. 85).

House of Commons (1984). *Compensation and Support for Victims of Crime: First Report of the Home Affairs Committee, together with Proceedings of the Committee, the Minutes of Evidence and Appendixes*. London, HMSO.

House of Commons (1987). *Fourth Report from the Home Affairs Committee, Session 1986–87: Contract Provision of Prisons*. London, HMSO (Cmnd 291, Sir Edward Gardner, Chairman).

Howell, J. C. (1972). 'A Comparison of Probation Officers and Volunteers'. Ph.D. thesis. Colorado, University of Colorado.

Humble, S. (1982). *Voluntary Action in the 1980s: a Summary of the Findings of a National Survey*. Berkhamsted, Volunteer Centre.

Hyman, H. M. and Tarrant, C. M. (1975). 'Aspects of American trial jury history', in R. J. Simon (ed.). *The Jury System in America*. Beverly Hills, Sage.

Illich, I. (1973). *Deschooling Society*. Harmondsworth, Penguin.

Illich, I. *et al*. (1977). *Disabling Professions*. London, Boyars.

Ingman, T. (1987). *The English Legal Process*. London, Financial Trading Publications.

Jackson, H. (1985). *Recruiting Volunteers*. London, HMSO (HORPU paper 31).

Jackson, R. H. (1979). *The Machinery of Justice in England*. Cambridge, Cambridge University Press.

Jacobs, J. (1969). *The Death and Life of Great American Cities*. New York, Random House.

James, J. T. L., Sloan, R. L. and Perry, R. P. (1977). 'The volunteer probation officer programme in Manitoba'. *Canadian Journal of Criminal Corrections*, 19, 95–104.

James, P. (1985). 'Day centres', in H. Walker and B. Beaumont (eds). *Working with Offenders*. London, Macmillan.

Jarvis, F. V. (1971). 'The Probation and After Care Service of England and Wales: an up-to-date approval'. *Offender Therapy Series, APTO Monographs*, 8–18.

Jarvis, F. V. (1980). *Probation Officers' Manual* (third edition). London, Butterworth.

Johnson, N. (1981). *Voluntary Social Services*. Oxford, Blackwell/Robertson.

Jones, S. (1986). *Policewomen and Equality*. Basingstoke, Macmillan.

Karpets, I. I. (1977). 'Principal directions and types of activity of the militia in the Soviet Union'. *International Review of Criminal Policy*, 33, 34–8.

Kinsey, R., Lea, J. and Young, J. (1986). *Losing the Fight against Crime*. Oxford, Blackwell.

Lacey, A. W. (1963). 'The role of voluntary effort in the after care of offenders'. Ph.D. thesis. London, London School of Economics and Political Science.

Latane, B. and Darley, J. (1970). *The Unresponsive Bystander*. New York, Appleton-Century-Crofts.

Leat, D. and Rankin, M. (1981). *A Survey of the Involvement of Volunteers with Probation and Aftercare Services in England and Wales*. Berkhamsted, Volunteer Centre.

Leon, C. (1987). 'The special constabulary: a historical view'. *Special Edition*, 1.6, 5–8.

Lewis, P. (1988). 'When cash is a drug'. *Community Care: Inside the Voluntary Sector*, 25 February.

Lowenberg, D. A. (1981). 'An integrated victim service model', in B. Galaway and J. Hudson (eds). *Perspectives on Crime Victims*. St Louis, C. V. Molsby.

Lubman, S. (1967). 'Mao and mediation: politics and dispute resolution in Communist China'. *California Law Review*, 55, 1284–359.

Lubman, S. (1969). 'Form and function in the Chinese criminal process'. *Columbia Law Review*, 69, 535–75.

McClenahan, C. A. (1987). 'Victim/witness services: Vancouver, British Columbia, Canada'. Paper to American Criminological Association Conference, Montreal.

MacDonald, W. F. (1976). 'Criminal justice and the victim: an introduction', in W. F. MacDonald (ed.). *Criminal Justice and the Victim*. Beverly Hills, Sage.

McKensie, I. (1984). 'Policing in Japan'. *Police Review*, 14 December, 2417–19.

McLachlan, P. (1988). 'How volunteers help victims'. Paper to Sixth International Symposium on Victimology, Jerusalem.

Maguire, M. and Corbett, C. (1987). *The Effects of Crime and the Work of Victim Support Schemes*. Aldershot, Gower.

Maguire, M. and Vagg, J. (1984). *The 'Watchdog' Role of Boards of Visitors*. London, Home Office.

Mather, F. C. (1959). *Public Order in the Age of the Chartists*. Manchester, Manchester University Press.

Mawby, R. I. (1979). *Policing the City*. Aldershot, Gower.

Mawby, R. I. (1985). 'Bystander responses to the victims of crime: is the Good Samaritan alive and well?'. *Victimology*, 10, 461–75.

Mawby, R. I. (1989). 'The voluntary sector's role in a mixed economy of criminal justice', in R. Matthews (ed.). *Privatizing Criminal Justice*. London, Sage.

Mawby, R. I. and Gill, M. L. (1987). *Crime Victims: Needs, Services and the Voluntary Sector*. London, Tavistock.

Mayhew, P., Clarke, R. V. G., Burrows, J. N., Hough, J. M. and Winchester, S. W. C. (1979). *Crime in the Public View*. London, HMSO (HORS no. 49).

Mellor, H. W. (1985). *The Role of Voluntary Organizations in Social Welfare*. London, Croom Helm.

Miller, W. R. (1977). *Cops and Bobbies: Police Authority in New York and London, 1830–1870*. Chicago, University of Chicago Press.

Milton, F. (1967). *The English Magistracy*. London, Oxford University Press.

Ministry of Justice (1982). *Correctional Institutions in Japan*. Tokyo, Corrections Bureau.

Moore, C. and Brown, J. (1981). *Community versus Crime*. London, Bedford Square Press.

Morgan, R. (1987). 'Consultation and police accountability', in R. I. Mawby (ed.). *Policing Britain*. Plymouth, Plymouth Polytechnic.

Morris, M. (1969). *Voluntary Work in the Welfare State*. London, Routledge & Kegan Paul.

Mounsey, S. C. (1973). 'Resistance to the use of volunteers in a probation setting: some practical issues discussed'. *Canadian Journal of Criminology and Corrections*, 15, 50–8.

Murgatroyd, S. (1987). *Volunteering in Hereford and Worcester Probation Service*. Worcester, Hereford and Worcester Probation Service.

Nakane, C. (1981). *Japanese Society*. Harmondsworth, Penguin.

NAVSS (1982). *Second Annual Report, 1981/82*. London, National Association of Victims Support Schemes.

NAVSS (1988). *Seventh Annual Report, 1986/87*. London, National Association of Victims Support Schemes.

Newman, O. (1972). *Defensible Space*. New York, Macmillan.

Newman, O. (1976). *Design Guidelines for Creating Defensible Space*. Washington, D.C., National Institute of Law Enforcement and Criminal Justice, GPO.

Newton, N. (1987). 'A special kind of watch'. *Police Review*, 27 February, 430–1.

O'Connor, D. M. (1964). 'Soviet People's Guards: an experiment with civic police'. New York, *University Law Review*, 39, 579–614.

Owings, C. (1969). *Women Police: a Study of the Development and Status of the Women Police Movement*. Montclair, NJ, Patterson Smith (reprint, original 1925).

Pahl, J. (1979). 'Refuges for battered women: social provision or social movement?'. *Journal of Voluntary Action Research*, 8, 25–35.

Pinchbeck, I. and Hewitt, M. (1973). *Children in English Society, 2: From the Eighteenth Century to the Children's Act 1948*. London, Routledge.

Pinker, R. (1986). 'Social welfare in Japan and Britain: a comparative view. Formal and informal aspects of welfare', in E. Oyen (ed.). *Comparing Welfare States and their Futures*. Aldershot, Gower.

Pirie, M. and Young, P. (1987). *The Future of Privatization*. London, Adam Smith Institute.

Pitts, J. (1988). *The Politics of Juvenile Crime*. London, Sage.

Pointing, J. and Maguire, M. (1988). 'Introduction: the rediscovery of the crime victim', in Maguire and Pointing, *Victims of Crime*. Milton Keynes, Open University Press.

Police Advisory Board for England and Wales (1976). *Report of the Working Party on the Special Constabulary*. London, HMSO.

Police Advisory Board for England and Wales (1981). *Report of the Second Working Party on the Special Constabulary*. London, HMSO.

Police Advisory Board for Scotland (1975). *Report of the Working Party on Special Constables*. Edinburgh, Scottish Office.

Poorkaj, H. and Bockerman, C. (1973). 'The impact of community volunteers on delinquency prevention'. *Sociology and Social Research*, 57, 335–41.

Quinne, C. and Bazalgette, J. (1979). *The Final Report of a Pilot Project Funded by the SSRC*. London, Grubb Institute.

Radzinowicz, L. (1956a). *A History of English Criminal Law and its Administration from 1750: 3: Cross Currents in the Movement for the Reform of the Police*. London, Stevens.

Radzinowicz, L. (1956b). *A History of English Criminal Law and its Administration from 1750: 2: The Clash Between Private Initiative and Public Interest in the Enforcement of Law*. London, Stevens.

Ralphs, Lady (1988). *The Victim in Court: Report of a Working Party*. London, NAVSS.

Reading, Lady (1967). *The Place of Voluntary Service in After Care*. London, HMSO (Second Report of Working Party).

Reiss, A. J. (1971). *Police and Public*. New Haven, Conn., Yale University Press.

Richards, K. (1977). *Training Volunteer Organizers*. London, National Institute for Social Work (Papers, 3).

Riddick, M. (1984). 'A voluntary associate in the probation service', in G. Darvill and B. Munday (eds). *Volunteers in the Personal Social Services*. London, Tavistock.

Ridley, J. and Currie, R. (1987). *Towards a Better Partnership: Social Workers and Volunteers*. Birmingham: British Association of Social Workers.

Rock, P. (1988). 'Government, victims and police in two countries'. *British Journal of Criminology*, 28, 44–66.

Rosenthal, T. (1964). *Thirty-Eight Witnesses*. New York, McGraw-Hill.

Ryan, M. (1978). *The Acceptable Pressure Group: A Case Study of the Howard League and RAP*. Aldershot, Gower.

Salas, L. (1979). *Social Control and Deviance in Cuba*. New York, Praeger.

Salas, L. (1985). 'The judicial system of post-revolutionary Cuba', in A. Podrogeck, C. J. Whelan and D. Khosla (eds). *Legal Systems and Social Systems*. London, Croom Helm.

Scarman, Lord (1981). *The Brixton Disorders: 10–12 April 1981*. London, HMSO (Cmnd 8427).

Schafer, S. (1960). *Restitution to Victims of Crime*. London, Stevens.

Scheier, I. H. (1970). 'The professional and the volunteer in probation: an emerging relationship'. *Federal Probation*, 34.12, 12–18.

Scheier, I. H. and Goter, L. P. (1969). *Using Volunteers in Court Settings: a Manual for Volunteer Probation Programmes*. Washington, DC, US Department of Health, Education and Welfare, Government Printing Office.

Schneider, A. L. and Schneider, P. R. (1981). 'Victim assistance programmes', in B. Galaway and J. Hudson (eds). *Perspectives on Crime Victims*. St Louis, C. V. Molsby.

Schwartz, I. A. (1971). 'Volunteers and professionals: a team in the correctional process'. *Federal Probation*, 35.3, 46–50.

Schwartz, R. D. and Miller, J. C. (1964). 'Legal evolution and societal complexity'. *American Journal of Sociology*, 70, 159–69.

Scioli, F. P. and Cook, T. J. (1976). 'How effective are volunteers?'. *Crime and Delinquency*, 22, 192–200.

Seth, R. (1961). *The Specials*. London, Victor Gollancz.

Shapland, J. (1988). 'Fiefs and peasants: accomplishing change for victims in the criminal justice system', in M. Maguire and J. Pointing (eds). *Victims of Crime*. Milton Keynes, Open University Press.

Sheard, J. (1986). *The Politics of Volunteering*. London, Advance.

Sherrott, R. (1983). 'Fifty volunteers', in S. Hatch (ed.). *Volunteers: Patterns, Meanings and Motives*. Berkhamsted, Volunteer Centre.

Sherwood, J. (1980). 'Auxiliary police units: popular but selective'. *Enforcement Journal*, 18.3, 5–7.

Shields, P. M., Chapman, C. W. and Wingard, D. R. (1983). 'Using volunteers in adult probation'. *Federal Probation*, 47.2, 57–64.

Shubert, A. (1981). 'Private initiative in law enforcement: associations for the prosecution of felons, 1744–1856', in V. Bailey (ed.), *Policing and Punishment in Nineteenth-Century Britain*. London, Croom Helm.

Simeral, I. (1916). *Reform Movements in Behalf of Children in England of the Early Nineteenth Century and the Agents of those Reforms*. New York.

Simon, R. J. (1980). *The Jury: Its Role in American Society*. Lexington, Mass., D.C. Heath.

Simon, S. (1987). 'Welfare or Rights? Two Local Responses to Victim Needs in the UK and USA'. Diploma in Criminology thesis. London, University of London.

Smith, B. L. (1985). 'Trends in the victims' rights movement and implications for future research'. *Victimology*, 10, 34–43.

Smith, D. (1986). 'The framework of law and policing practice', in J. Benyon and C. Bourn (eds). *The Police Powers, Procedures and Properties*. Oxford, Pergamon.

Smith, G. and Harris, R. (1982). 'Ideologies of need and the organization of social work departments'. *British Journal of Social Work*, 2.1, 27–45.

Smith, P. F. and Bailey, S. H. (1984). *The Modern English Legal System*. London, Sweet & Maxwell.

Smith, P. T. (1985). *Policing Victorian London*. Westport, Conn., Greenwood Press.

Spitzer, S. and Scull, A. T. (1977). 'Social control in historical perspective: from private to public responses to crime', in D. F. Greenberg (ed.). *Corrections and Punishment*. Beverly Hills, Sage.

Stead, P. J. (1985). *The Police of Britain*. London, Macmillan.

Steedman, C. (1984). *Policing the Victorian Community: The Formation of English Provincial Police Forces, 1856–80*. London, Routledge.

Stern, V. (1987). *Bricks of Shame: Britain's Prisons*. Harmondsworth, Penguin.

Stockdale, E. (1985). *The Probation Volunteer*. Berkhamsted, Volunteer Centre.

Sundeen, R. A. and Siegel, G. B. (1986). 'The uses of volunteers by the police'. *Journal of Police Science and Administration*, 14, 49–61.

Thatcher, M. (1981). 'Address to the WRVS National Conference'. London, Conservative Party Central Office.

Thomas, J. E. (1972). *The English Prison Officer Since 1850: A Study in Conflict*. London, Routledge.

Titmuss, R. M. (1971). *The Gift Relationship*. London, Allen & Unwin.

Todd, J. C. and Smith, R. (1983). 'Auxiliary volunteers stretch personnel resources'. *The National Sheriff*, 35, Aug.–Sept., 16–17.

United Nations (1951). *Probation and Related Measures*. New York, United Nations Department of Social Affairs.

US Department of Justice (1988). *Sourcebook of Criminal Justice Statistics – 1987*. Washington DC, US Government Printing Office.

Unkoviv, C. and Davis, J. R. (1969). 'Volunteers in probation and parole'. *Federal Probation*, 33.42, 41–5.

Van Dijk, J. (1985). 'Research and the victim movement in Europe', in Council of Europe. *Research on Crime Victims*. Strasbourg, Council of Europe.

Van Dijk, J. (1988). 'Ideological trends within the victims movement: an international perspective', in M. Maguire and J. Pointing (eds). *Victims of Crime*. Milton Keynes, Open University Press.

Vidosa, F. G. (1988). 'Creation, evolution, development: the Victim of Crime Support Office, Valencia (Spain)'. Paper to Sixth International Symposium on Victimology, Jerusalem.

Vizard, M. (1988). 'Volunteers – used or abused? A Probation View'. Paper to Probation Service Volunteers Conference, Exeter.

Vogel, E. F. (1971). 'Preserving order in the cities', in Lewis (ed.). *op. cit.*

Walklate, S. (1987). 'Public monitoring and police accountability'. Paper to British Criminology Conference, Sheffield.

Waller, I. (1988). 'International standards, national trail blazing and the next steps', in M. Maguire and J. Pointing (eds). *Victims of Crime*. Milton Keynes, Open University Press.

Walton, R. (1975). *Women in Social Work*. London, Routledge & Kegan Paul.

Walvin, J. (1982). *A Child's World*. Harmondsworth, Penguin.

Ward, K. (1984). 'Voluntary associates with the probation service', in G. Darvill and B. Munday (eds). *Volunteers in the Personal Social Services*. London, Tavistock.

White, S. and Nelson, D. (eds) (1986). *Communist Politics: a Reader*. London, Macmillan.

Willett, T. and Chitty, P. (1982). 'Auxiliary police in Canada – an overview'. *Canadian Police College Journal*, 6.3, 188–92.

Wolfenden, J. (1978). *The Future of Voluntary Organizations*. London, Croom Helm.

Wood, T. (1980). 'Staff, volunteer and client perceptions on the use of volunteers in probation'. *Canadian Journal of Criminology*, 2, 206–11.

Young, M. A. and Stein, J. H. (1983). *The Victim Service System: a Guide to Action*. Washington, DC, NOVA.

Younghusband, E. (1978). *Social Work in Britain 1950–75*. London, Allen & Unwin.

INDEX